EASY GUITAR

John Denver Anthology

Revised Edition

 For a comprehensive listing of Cherry Lane Music's songbooks, sheet music, instructional materials, videos and more, check out our entire catalog on the Internet.
Our home page address is: http://www.cherrylane.com

CONTENTS

In a career that has spanned more than two decades, John Denver has earned international acclaim as a songwriter, performer, actor, and humanitarian.

Henry John Deutschendorf, Jr. began his career in the 1960s as an aspiring folk musician in the clubs of Los Angeles. The son of a U.S. Air Force officer, John took his performing name from the premier Rocky Mountain city in the state where he eventually made his home.

His first major break came in the mid-60s when he was chosen from 250 other hopefuls as lead singer for the popular Chad Mitchell Trio, with whom he sang for two years. His songwriting talents became evident when Peter, Paul & Mary recorded his "Leaving On A Jet Plane," which became their first Number One hit.

Soon after, Denver himself was zooming up the pop charts with a string of hits, including "Take Me Home, Country Roads," "Rocky Mountain High," "Sunshine On My Shoulders," "Annie's Song," "Back Home Again" and "Thank God I'm A Country Boy," and solidifying his position as one of the top pop stars of the 70s. Many of his songs tapped into the growing appreciation and concern for the environment, which has continued as a matter of major importance for Denver and for us all.

His popularity since the early 70s may be measured in record sales that few other artist have achieved, including fourteen gold and eight platinum albums in the U.S. alone. He also has many gold and platinum sales overseas, in countries such as Australia, Germany, and the United Kingdom. The album JOHN DENVER'S GREATEST HITS is still one of the largest-selling albums in the history of RCA Records, with worldwide sales of over ten million copies. He is one of the top recording artists in the sales history of the music industry.

"My music and all my work stem from the conviction that people everywhere are intrinsically the same," Denver says of the universality of music. "When I write a song, I want to take the personal experience or observation that inspired it and express it in as universal a way as possible. I'm a global citizen. I think we all are—at least we've all got to start thinking that way. I want to work in whatever I do—my music, my writing, my performing, my commitments, my home and personal life—in a way that is directed towards a world in balance, a world that creates a better quality of life for all people."

JOHN DENVER: Reflections

Following are John's thoughts on such memorable songs as "Annie's Song," "Leaving On Jet Plane," "Rocky Mountain High," "Take Me Home, Country Roads," and "Sunshine On My Shoulders," as well as many others found in this anthology.

Annie's Song

"Annie's Song" is my most popular song around the world, if not the most famous. It was written after we had been through a particularly difficult time and had come together again, in many ways closer than ever before. We really felt together and much closer from the experiences we'd been through. One day I was skiing, and I'd just finished a run that was totally exhilarating. It was an incredible physical experience. I skied right down to the lift, got on the chair and was off and up the mountain again, my thighs burning and still in the process of catching my breath. I looked out at the mountains I love, and the Colorado sky was a blue color you can only see from this altitude—my favorite color, I might add. The deep green of the trees against the white of the snow, the colorful outfits the people were wearing, the sounds of the lift as it goes over each tower, and birds singing, and laughter, and the smell of the clean, fresh air out there in the wilderness—all these things were going through my mind and it was all beautiful. It filled me completely.

I began thinking about other things that are like that for me, and my first thought was of the woman I had fallen in love with again, and how she filled me so completely. Then I started thinking of other things—things in nature. And in the ten minutes it takes to go from the bottom of the Bell Mountain lift to the top, I had written "Annie's Song." I had the melody in my head, and I knew the chords on the guitar. I skied down to the bottom of the hill, raced home, picked up my guitar and played it. Noel Stookey of Peter, Paul and Mary said that sometimes he didn't feel so much like the writer, but rather the instrument of that which wants to be written. That's what this felt like to me. "Annie's Song" is a song for all lovers and, in its deepest sense, a prayer to the love in us all.

Back Home Again

"Back Home Again" has to do with spending so much time on the road, and then coming home and knowing where you are and knowing that place as HOME. I remember coming home one day and sitting up in my loft, watching that storm come across the valley, hearing Annie working down in the kitchen and feeling so good, so safe and warm and at peace. I thought about what it must be like for anyone who comes back to the place that is home to them, no matter how long they've been gone, and, as always, to say it in as personal and universal way as possible and capture the feeling of that return and that peace. I couldn't have stopped the song from coming if I'd tried.

Calypso

"Calypso" was written for my friend, Captain Jacques Yves Cousteau—a true inspiration in my life and, I'm sure, for many others—and for Madame Cousteau. I had the pleasure and privilege of meeting Captain Cousteau and spending some time on board the Calypso as part of a television special. The chorus of the song came to me in the first free moments I had on board. Then I began struggling with the verses, wanting to say all I felt about this man and his work, ship and crew, and the importance of the world that he opened up for us. I just couldn't find the words for it all. Finally, one day, long after leaving Calypso, back home in Aspen, I just gave up and went skiing. After a couple of runs this great tension came over me. I had to get back and work on the song. I jumped in the Jeep and headed home, and in the 20 minutes it took to get there I had worked out the rest of the song. This is an example I use when I tell people about being the instrument of that which wants to be written. Sometimes you have to get yourself out of the way and just let it happen. I love "Calypso." It's a song of celebration and commitment to making a difference and a contribution to the quality of life on this planet. I share that commitment. It's why I sing.

The Eagle And The Hawk

"The Eagle And The Hawk" was written for a television show. It starred Nell Newman, the daughter of Joanne Woodward and Paul Newman, and another old friend, Morley Nelson. Morley lives in Boise, Idaho, and knows more about birds of prey than any man in the world. The song came out of the experience of holding a young golden eagle on my arm, and getting a sense of the power and majesty of this bird of prey and why it has been a symbol of every civilization in the history of man. Oh, to be an eagle, to fly like an eagle.

Fly Away

"Fly Away" was written about someone whose life just hasn't come together yet—a person who is living in a space of unhappiness, unfulfillment and dissatisfaction; lost in longing for a lover; dreaming of having children, but never willing to take responsibility for the things she wants and yet not quite content in her fantasies. So, within the fantasy, she always flies away—her mind flies away but not her heart.

Follow Me

"Follow Me" is the second song of what I call my "Jet Plane Trilogy." ("Leaving On A Jet Plane" and "Goodbye Again" are the first and third.) I suppose that my greatest longing was for someone to be with—to be with me in all that I am called to do. At the time I wrote this song I had found Annie, but I simply couldn't afford to take her on the road with me. I believe that I knew even then that that was not what she wanted anyway. Mary Travers of Peter, Paul and Mary saw the self-centeredness of the song, thinking it sexist, and changed the last line to "take my hand and I will follow too." I'm not completely sure it's accurate in my case, and I'm afraid I'm becoming more and more self-centered. I'm still looking for someone to "take my hand and say you'll follow me."

For Baby (For Bobbie)

"For Baby (For Bobbie)" is the first song that I wrote with the Mitchell Trio, and was the first song of mine ever recorded by anyone (the Mitchell Trio, Peter, Paul and Mary, and Bobby Darin). It was written for a girl named Bobbie, who I had fallen in love with once upon a time, when I was first starting out in the world and trying to do something with my music. The song fits her well and is a very accurate representation of the shape and form of our love at the time—all that it was, and all that it wasn't. Mary Travers (of Peter, Paul and Mary) heard the song differently and sang it as a love song for her daughter. It's great that a song can be appreciated on different levels like that. So, it's "For Bobbie"—a love song between a man and a woman (not quite yet a man and a woman), and "For Baby"—a love song from a woman to a newborn child. How wonderful.

Goodbye Again

"Goodbye Again" is the third of what I called earlier "The Jet Plane Trilogy." Annie and I were living in Aspen and we were in a much better position to afford her traveling with me when she wanted to, but Annie didn't much like to travel. She didn't like the one-night stands, the pressures of so much attention, of constantly having strangers around and having to be "on" all the time. She wanted to be home with our family and friends. Consequently, "Goodbye Again" was an ongoing, frustrating, and unhappy part of our lives. I can't imagine it having been any other way, unfortunately.

I'd Rather Be A Cowboy (Lady's Chains)

"I'd Rather Be A Cowboy (Lady's Chains)" is another of my favorite songs. Quite honestly, I long for a simpler life. It would be very easy for me to spend more time at home, more time in the mountains. Consequently, I think of what life would be like under different circumstances. What if I had that cabin in the mountains, and it was my woman who wanted life a little closer to the fast lane? Would I—could I love her just enough to let her go? I think so.

I'm Sorry

"I'm Sorry" looks at women and an aspect of their lives that was becoming more and more prevalent at the time the song was written. I remember seeing the cover story in both Time and Newsweek addressing the number of women who were leaving seemingly solid, committed relationships, even marriages, to create new lives for themselves. They were finding that they weren't happy, and that the things that were supposed to be the "be all and end all" of their lives were somehow not that—that, in fact, they felt incomplete and unfulfilled. Suddenly, within the women's liberation movement, they began to find the courage to say, "Well, maybe I don't have to be stuck here, and I'm going to take a step for myself and take a different look, and perhaps create a better life for myself." It was scary and dangerous thinking for many of us, and I thought about what it must be like to be the man in that situation, with or without children, when the woman really wants to take a break and get away to make her own life. Suddenly, he is forced to look at some things that he didn't take seriously before. Now, in his pain, all of the things that built up to this particular moment have a deeper meaning. Now, what else can you say?

Leaving On A Jet Plane

"Leaving On A Jet Plane" was initially called "Oh Babe I Hate To Go." Milt Okun is responsible for that title change—I shall be forever grateful to him. The song resulted from my way of life at that time. I was working with the Mitchell Trio and lived on the road. Either I stayed where the last concert was, or I'd go to the next concert city a bit early. I didn't have a home, or even a room somewhere to pile my things. Everything was in storage in California and I lived out of suitcases on the road—always leaving on a jet plane. I was terribly lonely, and I longed for someone to "hold me like you'll never let go." And somehow in my longing, I was able to express the reality of what was going on in a lot of other lives—the lives of young men and women going off to war, leaving home and family, perhaps unsure of what they were doing and not knowing if they would ever return. Isn't it funny how in the expression of your deepest feelings, you can say more than you ever imagined for someone else?

Matthew

"Matthew" was written for my father's family. My grandfather Deutschendorf came to the United States when he was twelve years old. He settled in Oklahoma and raised a family there—a family of twelve children. They grew up during the Depression years, a very difficult time in what is always a most difficult life. The thing that I remembered most from our visits to the Deutschendorf farm was the family spirit, the laughter, and the faith. The epitome of that was my Uncle Dean, who was the second youngest of Dad's brothers. I went on my first wheat harvest with Dean and learned a great deal from him. He was killed in a car accident when he was just twenty-one, and one day, thinking about him and the family, I wrote this song.

My Sweet Lady

There are songs I've written that turned out to be prophetic to a degree. This is one of those songs. I know a part of the reality occurred in my life long after I wrote the song, and I believe that some of it is yet to come true Oh, to love like this.

Poems, Prayers And Promises

"Poems, Prayers And Promises" is one of my very favorite songs. I sometimes feel as if I wrote the song before I could possibly have known what I was talking about. And yet I'm sure I did, if only intuitively. It's a song that comes from a very mellow space of family and friends, sitting around enjoying each other and enjoying life in a way that has no time attached to it—no urgency and no frustration, no resentment and no regrets. It's a peaceful time of being together and sharing the things that you feel very deeply, that you can't share with just anybody. And yet, within the sharing, there are things that come up that can't be expressed and the sense that everyone is feeling those things, too. How wonderful life is in moments like this, when you know you are not alone.

Rocky Mountain High

"Rocky Mountain High" was written during the first summer we lived in the Rocky Mountains. I was starting to go camping and fishing, and doing other things that I'd wanted to do all my life, and in the place where I most wanted to be. Everything was new and full of possibility, and I was so happy. I found some new friends and lost an old friend—killed on my motorcycle when he and his wife were visiting us over one weekend. Within that personal framework, there was also a big controversy going on about trying to get the 1972 Winter Olympics in Colorado. One night on a camping trip to watch the Perseid meteor shower, when it was literally "raining fire in the sky," I started writing this very personal song of my rebirth.

Sunshine On My Shoulders

"Sunshine On My Shoulders" has an interesting background. There was a movie being made at that time and I was asked to write a song for it. The movie had to do with two people who were going to die, and somehow they knew they were going to die, and the film was about how they spent their last day together. In one of the scenes they were at the beach, laughing and playing in the water, and then making love. And yet there was this overriding sense of sadness through it all. I wrote the song in Minnesota at the time I call late winter, early spring. It was a dreary day, gray and slushy. The snow was melting and it was too cold to go outside and have fun, but God, you're ready for spring. You want to get outdoors again and you're waiting for that sun to shine, and you remember how sometimes just the sun itself can make you feel good. And in that very melancholy frame of mind I wrote "Sunshine On My Shoulders."

Take Me Home, Country Roads

The first album that had great success for me was an album called Poems, Prayers & Promises, and the song that really made that album a success is one that I wrote with two friends, Bill and Taffy (Nivert) Danoff, from Starland Vocal Band. I met them at a place called The Cellar Door in Washington, D.C., when I was working with the Mitchell Trio and later when I started performing on my own. When I first had the opportunity to be a headliner at The Cellar Door, they asked me who I wanted for an opening act. I asked about having Bill and Taffy, who called themselves Fat City. They came and opened the shows for me. The first night we were together we went back to their place after closing, just to visit, see what was going on and enjoy being together. We had a bunch of songs we wanted to show each other. One of the songs was one they had started and were unable to complete. It was a song called "Take Me Home, Country Roads." In the wee hours of the morning, sometime between Christmas and New Year's Eve, in their basement apartment in Washington, D.C., we wrote "Take Me Home, Country Roads." It became my first Number One record.

Annie's Song

Words and Music by John Denver

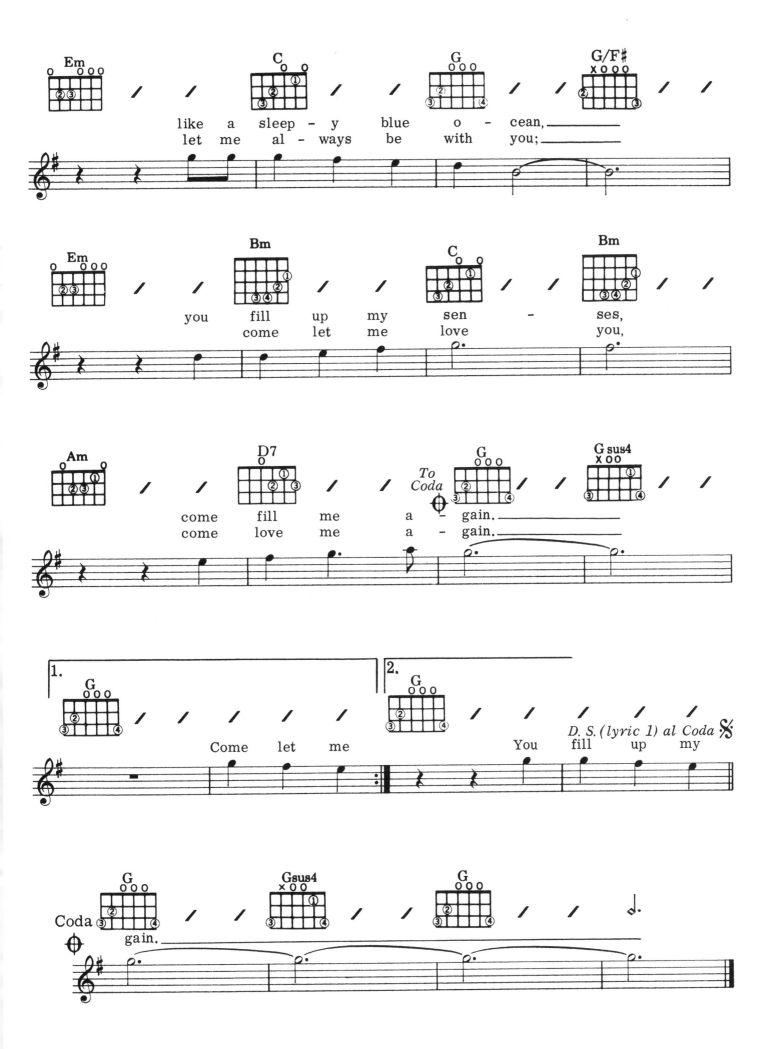

Autograph

Words and Music by John Denver

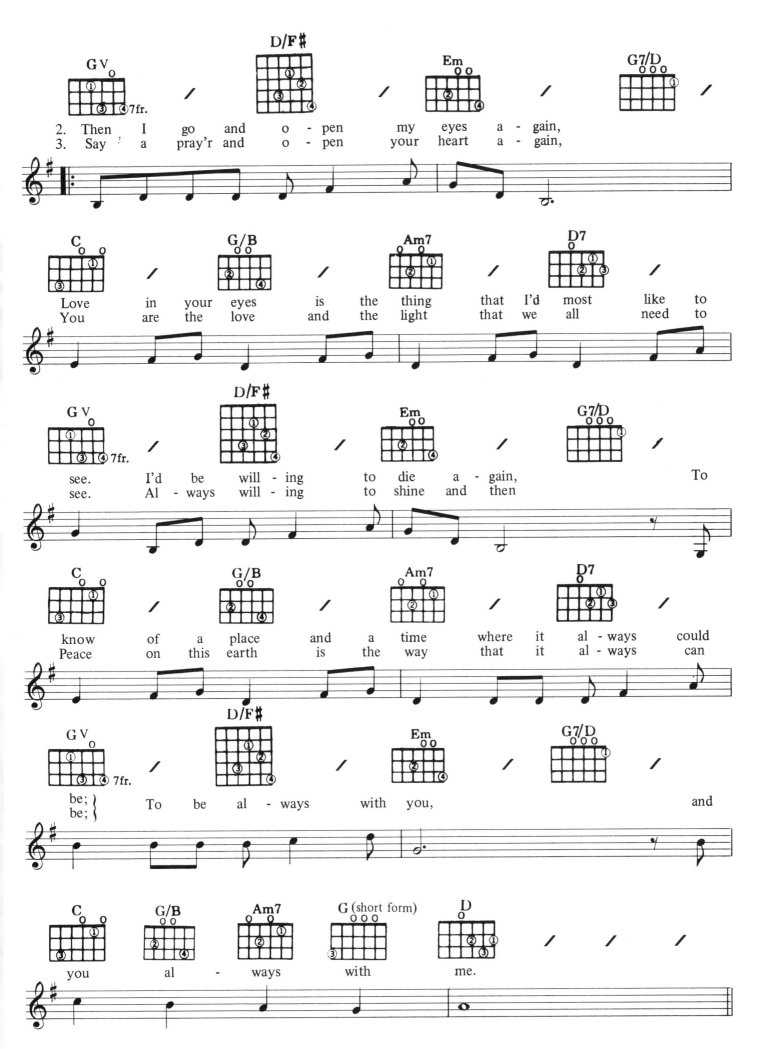

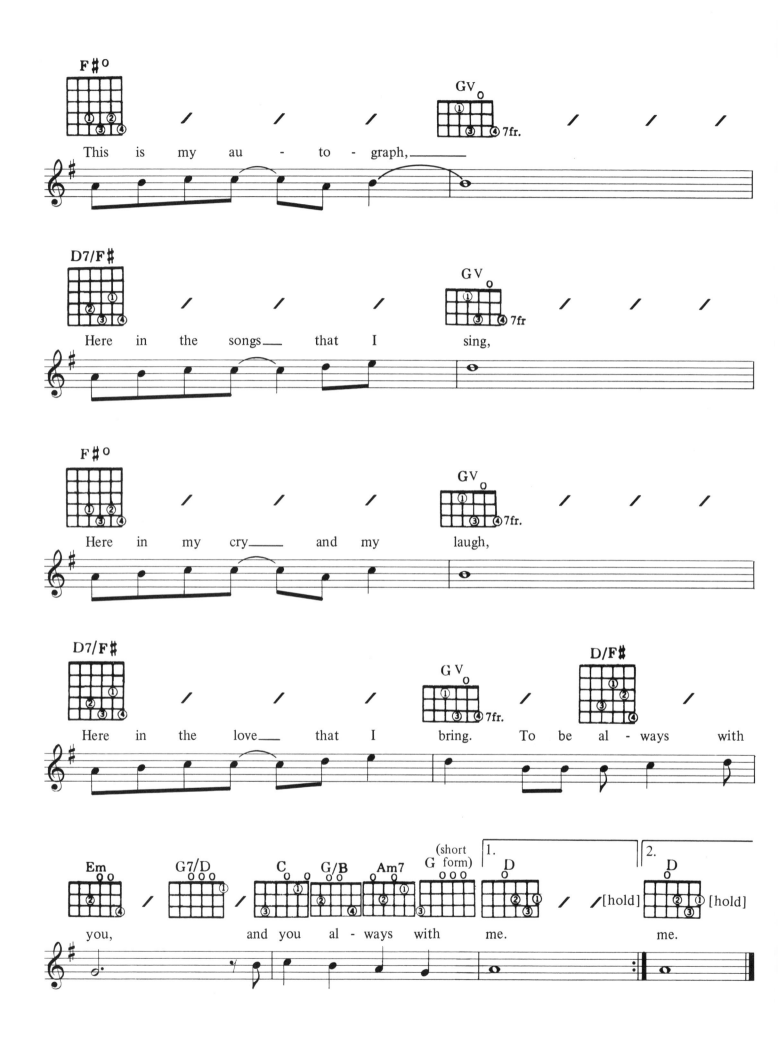

Back Home Again

Words and Music by John Denver

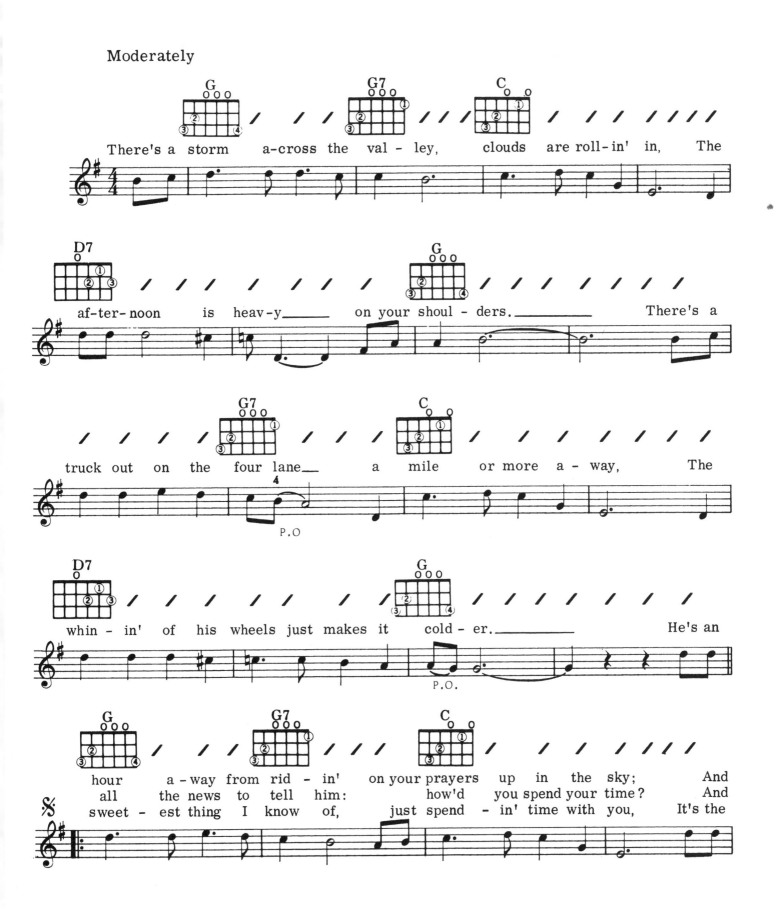

13

D7

ten days on the road____ are bare - ly gone._____
what's the lat - est thing____ the neigh-bors say?_____
lit - tle things that make____ a house a home._____

G

There's a
And your
Like a

G7

fire___ soft - ly burn - ing
moth - er called last Fri - day;
fire___ soft - ly burn - ing

C

sup - per's on the stove___ But it's the
"Sun - shine" made her cry,___ And you
and sup - per on the stove___ And the

D7

light in your eyes that makes him warm._____
felt the ba - by move just yes - ter - day._____
light in your eyes that makes me warm._____

G

Chorus

C   D7   G   G7

Hey, it's good to be back home a - gain;_____

C   D7   G

Some - times this old farm feels like a long - lost

14

friend. Yes 'n' hey, it's good to be back home a-

1. gain._____ There's

2. gain._____ And

oh, the time that I can lay this tired old bod-y down and

feel your fin-gers feath-er soft up-on me._____ The

kiss-es that I live for, the love that lights my way, The

D. S. and fade on Chorus

hap-pi-ness that liv-in' with you brings me._____ It's the

Ballad Of The St. Anne's Reel

Words and Music by David Mallett

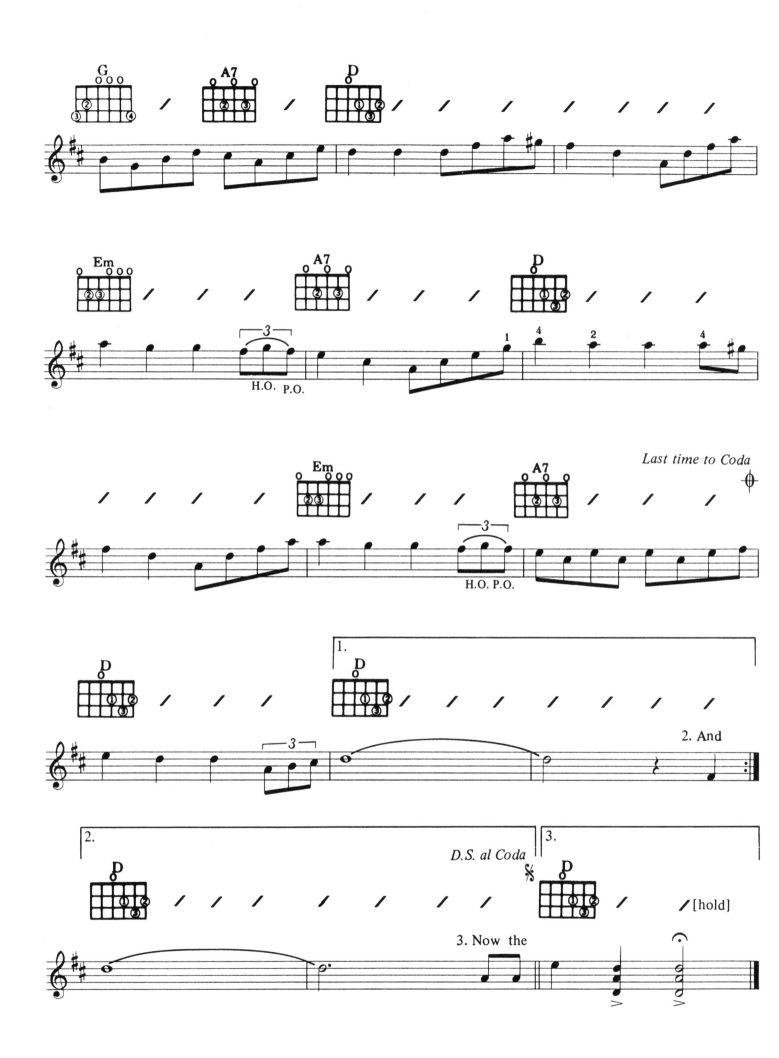

Calypso

Words and Music by John Denver

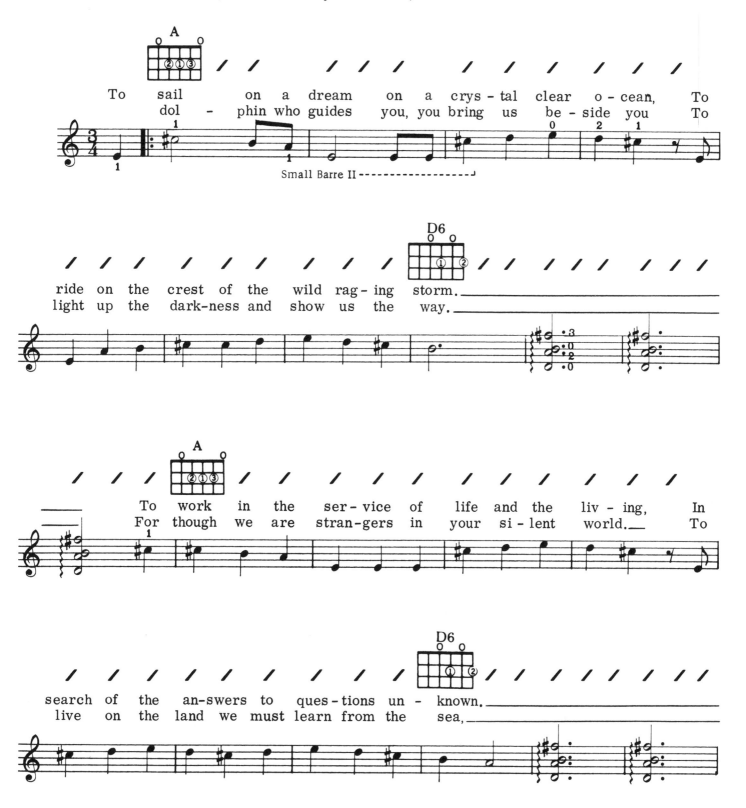

To be part of the move-ment and part of the grow-ing
To be true as the tide____ and free as a wind-swell,

Part of be - gin - ning to un - der - stand.____
Joy - ful and lov - ing in let - ting it be:

[Harmonics on 12th fret if desired.]

Aye,____ Ca - lyp - so, the plac - es you've

been to, The things that you've shown us, the sto - ries you

tell! Aye,____ Ca - lyp - so, I sing to your spir - it, The

22

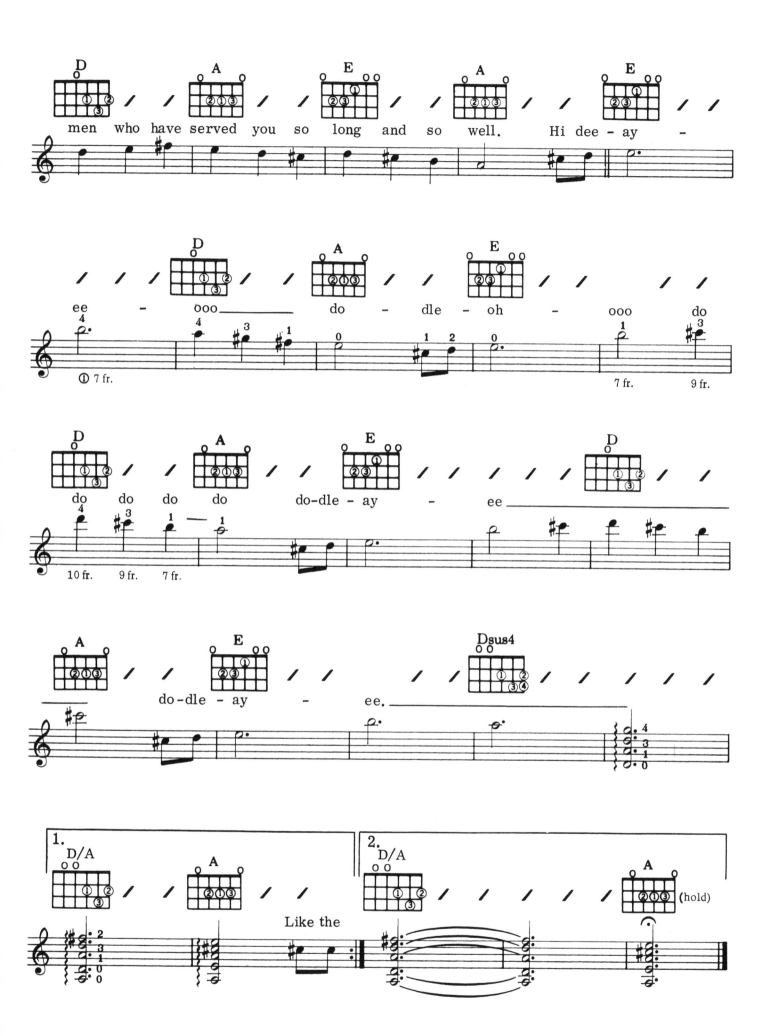

Dreamland Express

Words and Music by John Denver

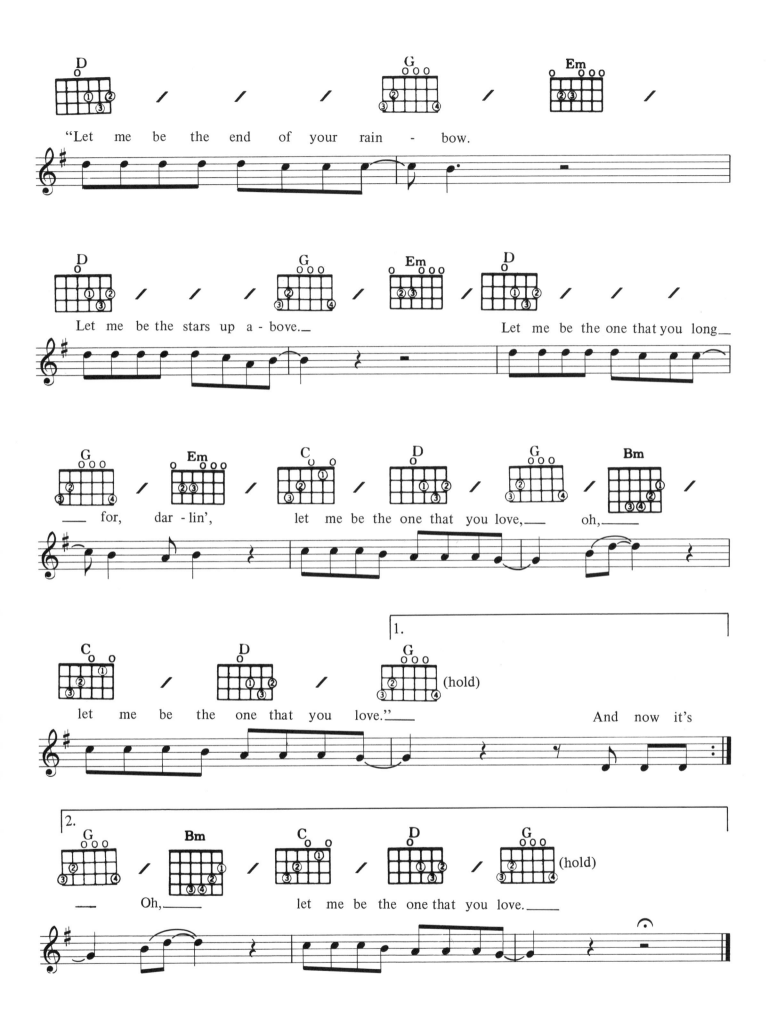

The Eagle And The Hawk

Words by John Denver
Music by John Denver and Mike Taylor

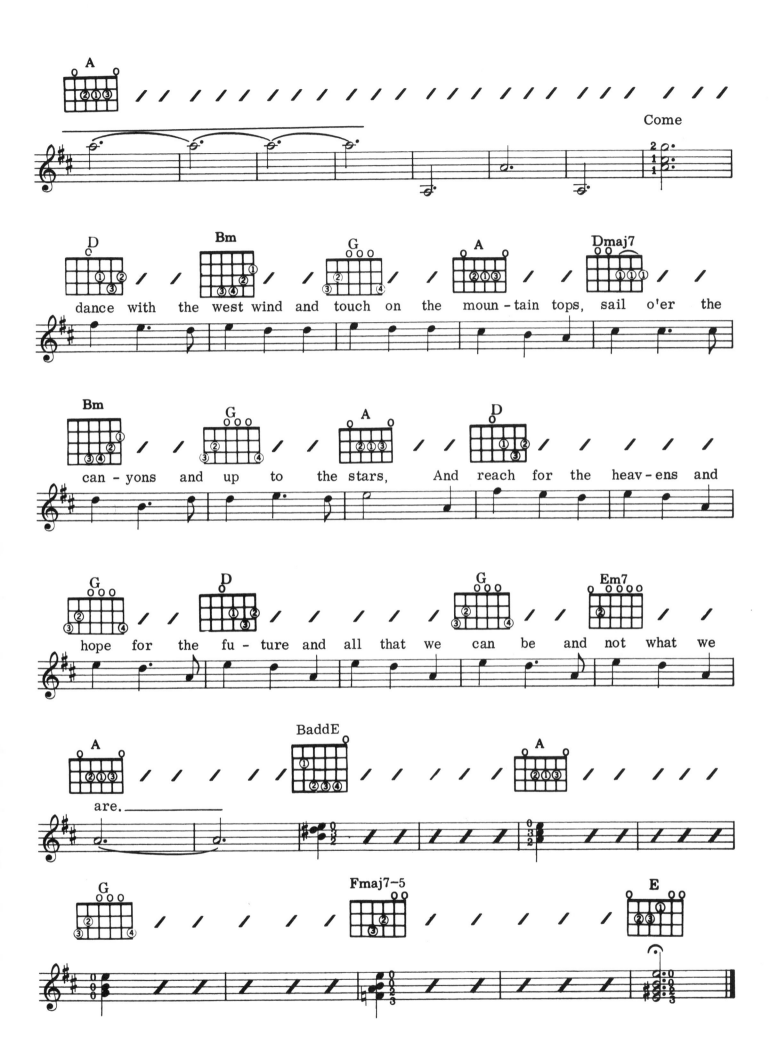

Eagles And Horses (I'm Flying Again)

Words by Joe Henry and John Denver
Music by John Denver

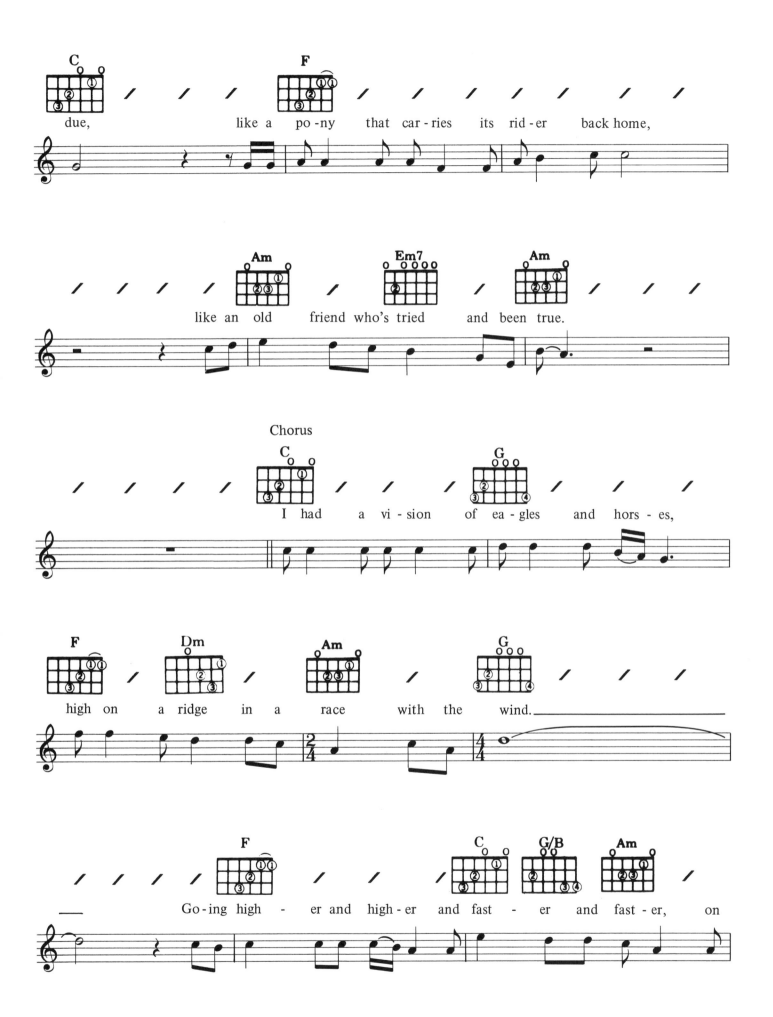

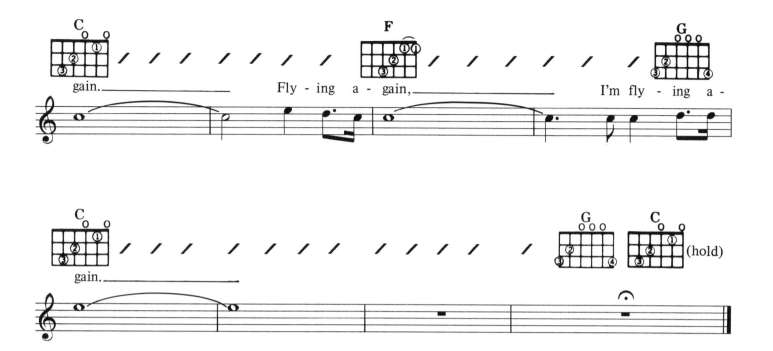

gain._____ Fly - ing a - gain,_____ I'm fly - ing a -

gain._____ (hold)

2. Eagles inhabit the heavenly heights;
   They know neither limit nor bound.
   They're the guardian angels of darkness and light;
   They see all and hear every sound.
   My spirit will never be broken or caught,
   For the soul is a free-flying thing,
   Like an eagle that needs neither comfort nor thought
   To rise up on glorious wings. *(To Chorus)*

3. My body is merely the shell of my soul,
   But the flesh must be given its due,
   Like a pony that carries its master back home,
   Like an old friend who's tried and been true.
   My spirit will never be broken or caught,
   For the soul is a free flying thing,
   Like an eagle that needs neither comfort nor thought
   To rise up on glorious wings. *(To Chorus)*

The Flower That Shattered The Stone

Words and Music by John Jarvis and Joe Henry

As the riv-er___ runs free-ly, the moun-tain does_ rise. Let me touch with my fin-gers and see with my_ eyes. In the hearts of the chil-dren, a pure love still grows,___ like a bright star in heav-en that lights our way_ home, like the flow-er___ that shat-tered the stone._

1.

2. (hold)

Follow Me

Words and Music by John Denver

To Coda

D   **D7**   **G**   **Am7**

me.   Fol-low me___ up and down___ all the

G   **C**   **G**   **C**   **D7**

way and all a - round,__ take my hand_ and say you'll fol-low me._

G   **G**   **D**

It's   long been on my mind,__ you know it's

You see, I'd like to share my life___ with you and

C   **G**   **Em**   **D**

been a long, long time, I'll try to find the way that I can

show you things I've seen, __ plac - es that I'm go - ing to, __

C   **D**   **C**

make you un - der - stand the way I feel a - bout_

plac - es where_ I've been, to have you there be - side_

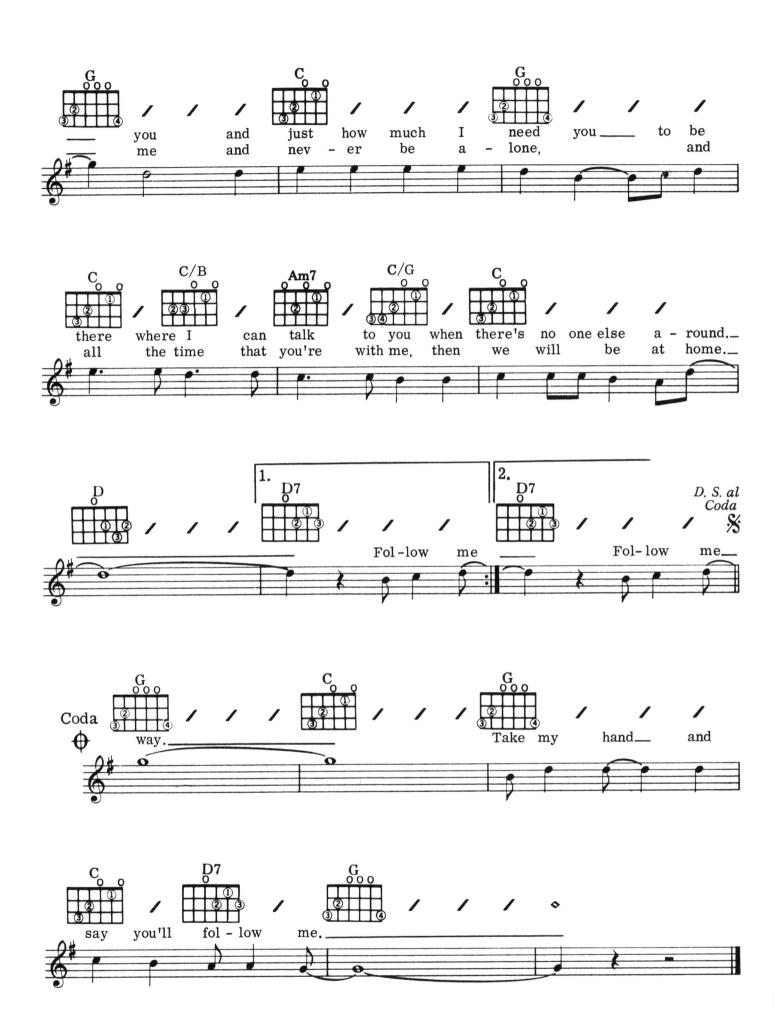

Fly Away

Words and Music by John Denver

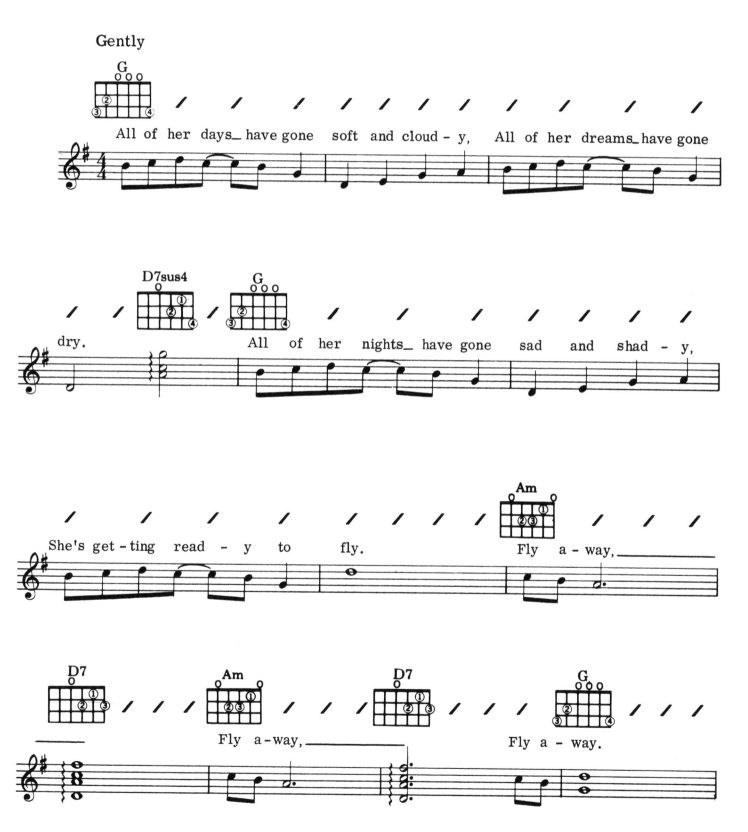

D7sus4

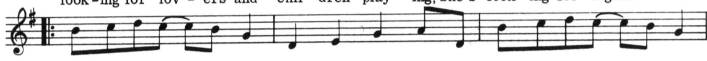

G

Life in the cit - y can make you cra - zy For sounds of the sand__ and the
look-ing for lov-ers and chil-dren play-ing, She's look-ing for signs__ of the

D7sus4   G

sea.   Life in a high - rise can make you hun - gry For
spring.   She lis-tens for laugh-ter and sounds of danc-ing, She

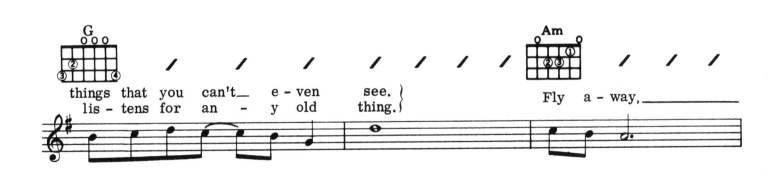

G   Am

things that you can't__ e - ven see.   Fly a - way,__
lis - tens for an - y old thing.

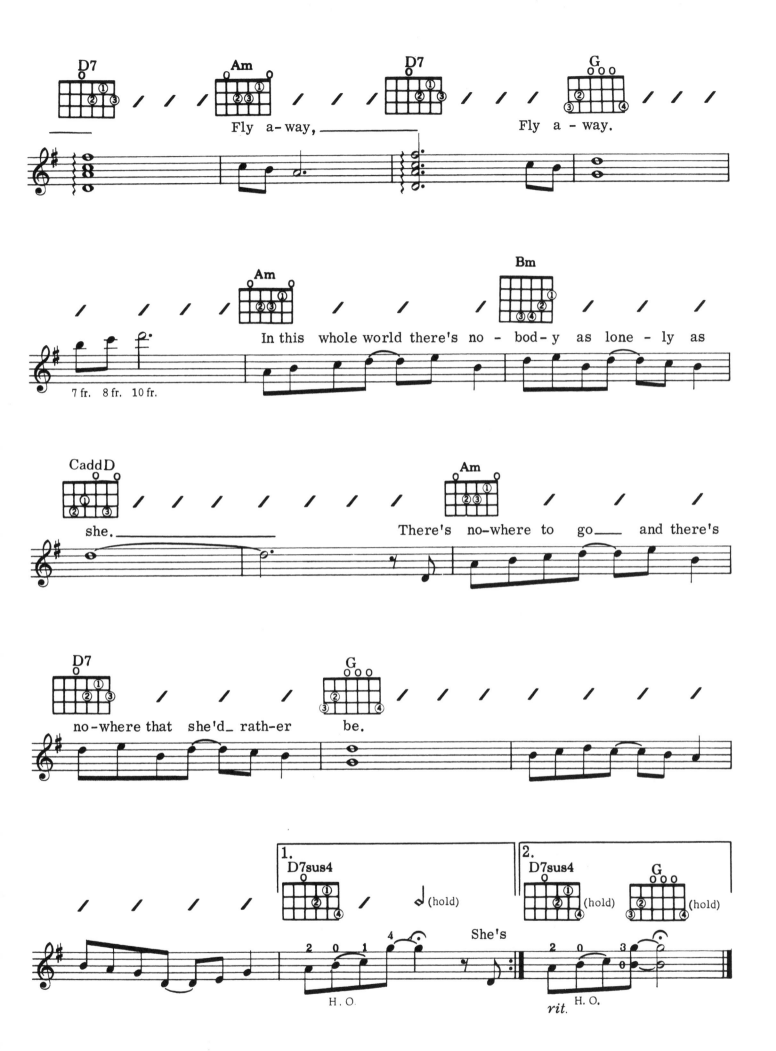

For Baby (For Bobbie)

Words and Music by John Denver

I'll walk in the rain by your side,
I'll cling to the warmth of your tiny hands.
I'll do anything to help you understand
And I'll love you more than anybody can.

And the wind will whisper your name to me,
Little birds will sing along in time.
Leaves will bow down when you walk by
And morning bells will chime.

Garden Song

Words and Music by David Mallett

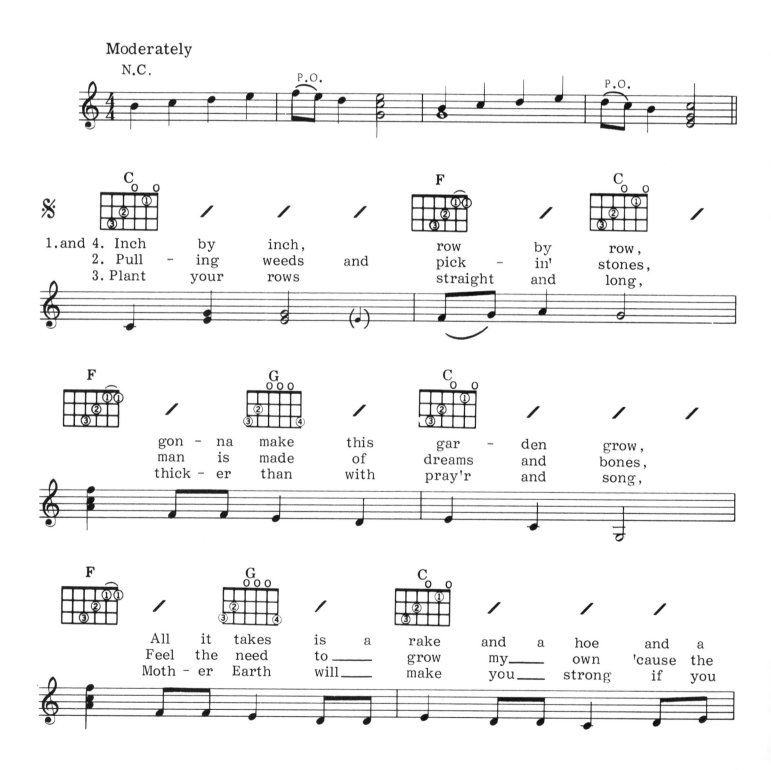

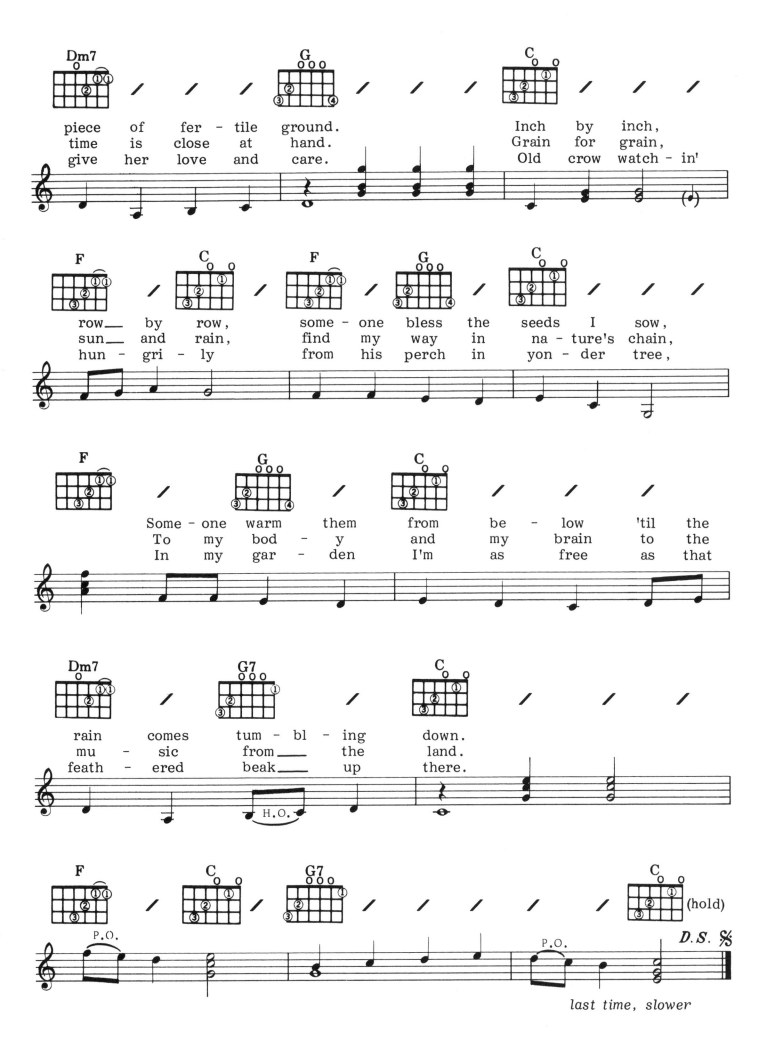

last time, slower

Grandma's Feather Bed

Words and Music by Jim Connor

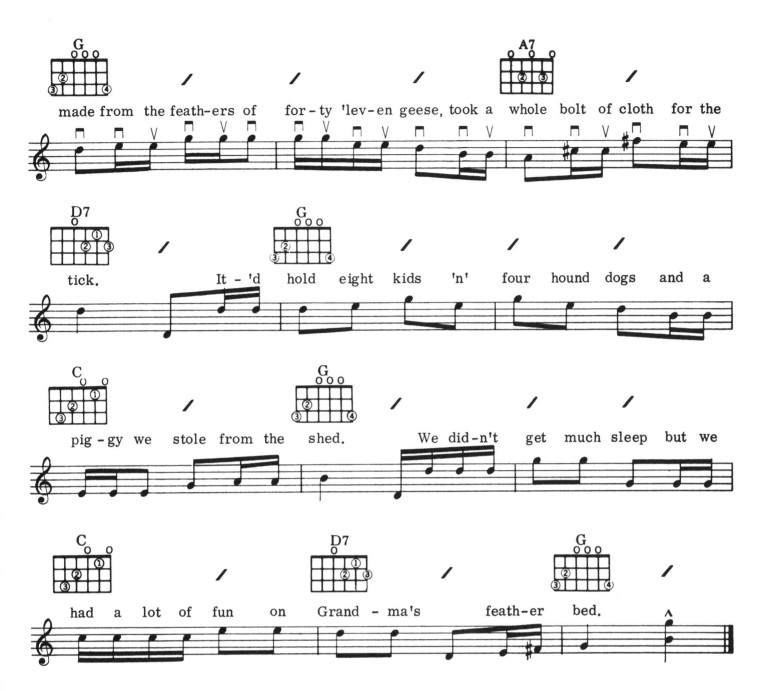

2. After supper we'd sit around the fire,
   The old folks'd spit and chew,
   Pa would talk about the farm and the war,
   And Granny'd sing a ballad or two.

   I'd sit and listen and watch the fire
   Till the cobwebs filled my head,
   Next thing I'd know I'd wake up in the mornin'
   In the middle of the old feather bed.
   (Chorus)

3. Well, I love my Ma, I love my Pa,
   I love Granny and Grandpa, too,
   I been fishin' with my uncle, rassled with my cousin,
   I even kissed Aunt Lou ooo!

   But if I ever had to make a choice,
   I guess it oughta be said
   That I'd trade 'em all plus the gal down the road
   For Grandma's feather bed.
   (Chorus)

For You

Words and Music by John Denver

48

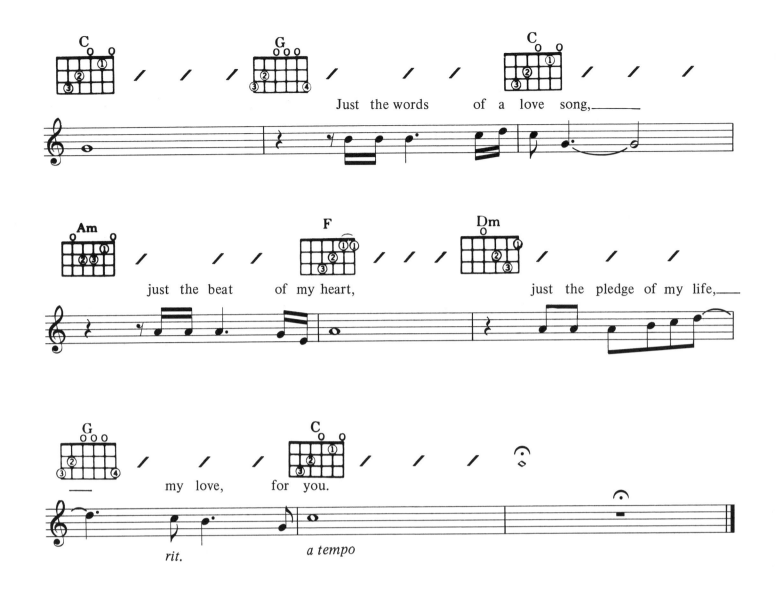

Just the words of a love song,_____

just the beat of my heart, just the pledge of my life,____

_____ my love, for you.

rit.   a tempo

2. Just to sit by your window,
   Just to touch in the night,
   Just to offer a prayer each day for you.
   Just to long for your kisses,
   Just to dream of your sighs,
   Just to know that I'd give my life
      for you. *(To Chorus)*

3. Just to wake up each morning,
   Just to you by my side,
   Just to know that you're never really far away.
   Just a reason for living,
   Just to say I adore,
   Just to know that you're here in my heart
      to stay. *(To Chorus)*

Goodbye Again

Words and Music by John Denver

Slowly, with a double time feeling

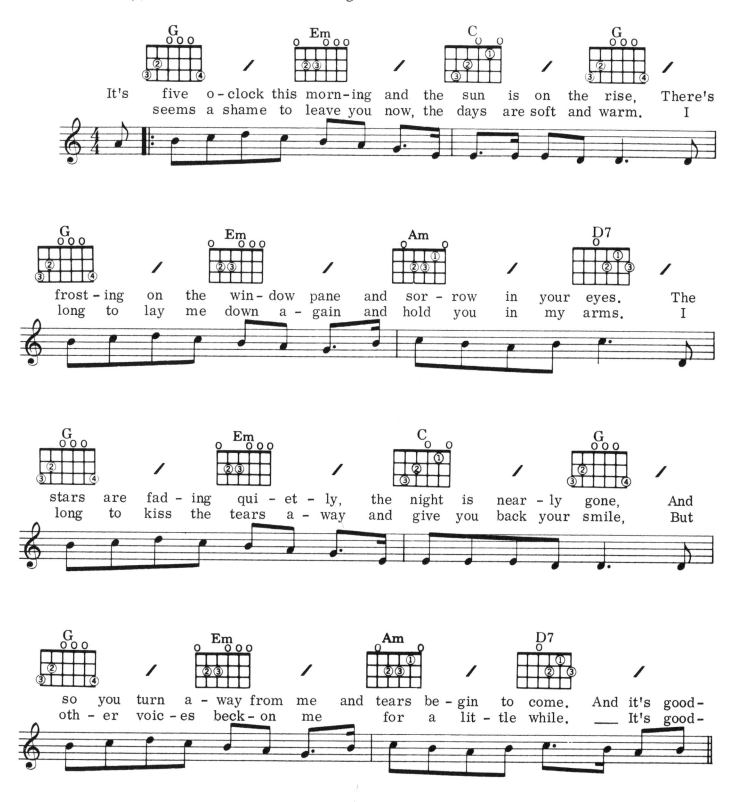

51

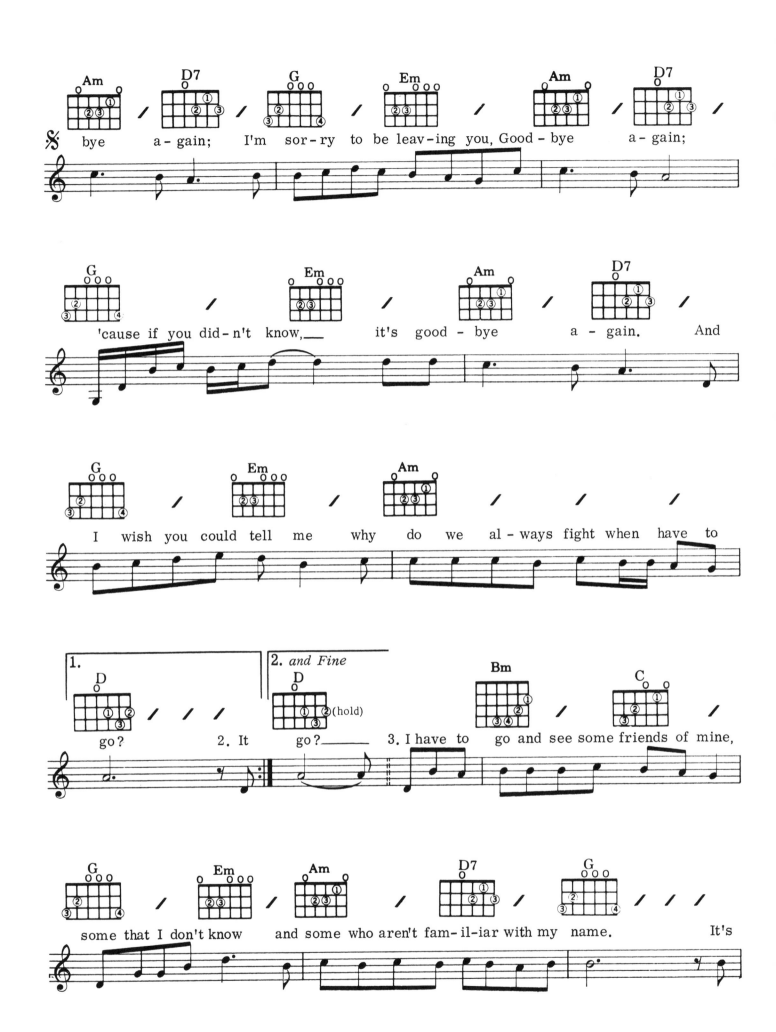

Am   D7   G   Em   Am   D7
bye a-gain; I'm sor-ry to be leav-ing you, Good-bye   a-gain;

G   Em   Am   D7
'cause if you did-n't know,___ it's good-bye   a-gain.   And

G   Em   Am
I wish you could tell me   why do we al-ways fight when have to

1.
D
go?   2. It

2. and Fine
D
go?_____ 3. I have to

Bm   C
go and see some friends of mine,

G   Em   Am   D7   G
some that I don't know   and some who aren't fam-il-iar with my name.   It's

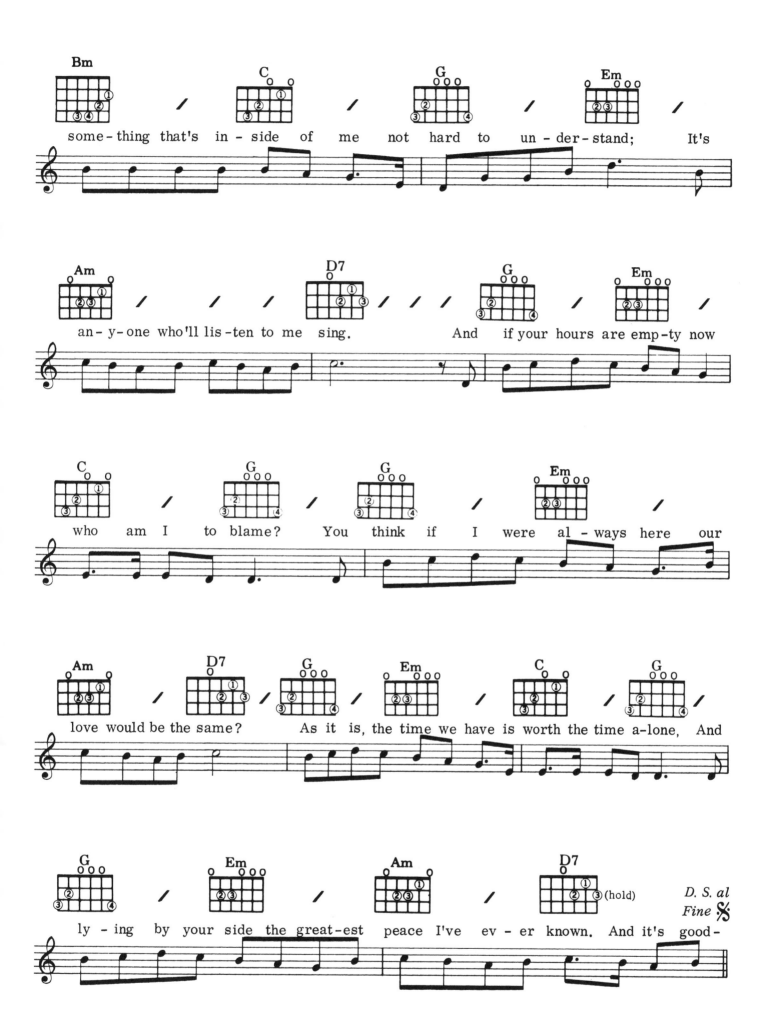

I Guess He'd Rather Be In Colorado

Words and Music by Bill Danoff and Taffy Nivert Danoff

I Want To Live

Words and Music by John Denver

voic - es   raised   as   one.
pas - sa - ges   and   home.

I   want   to

live,   I   want   to   grow,   I   want   to   see,   I   want   to   know,   I   want   to

share   what   I   can   give.   I   want   to   be,   I   want   to   live._____

1.

_____   Have   you   ____   For   the

2.

work - er   and   the   war - ri - or,   the   lov - er   and   the   liar;   For   the

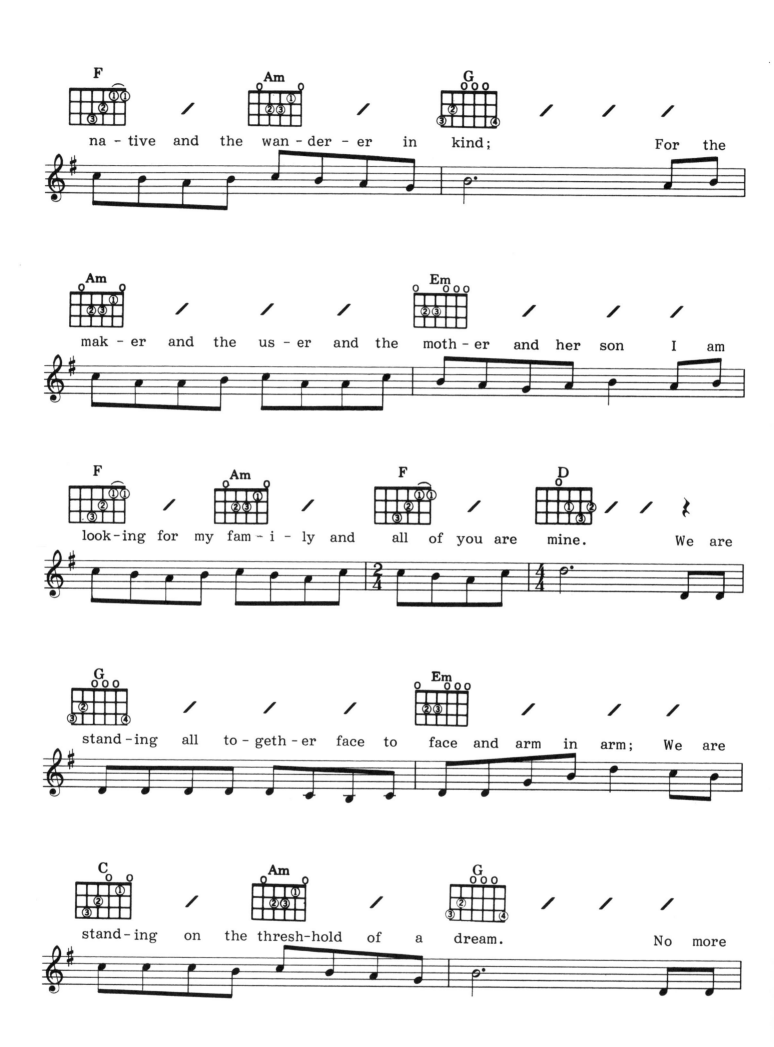

native and the wan-der-er in kind;   For the

mak-er and the us-er and the moth-er and her son   I am

look-ing for my fam-i-ly and   all of you are   mine.   We are

stand-ing all to-geth-er face to   face and arm in arm;   We are

stand-ing on the thresh-hold of   a   dream.   No more

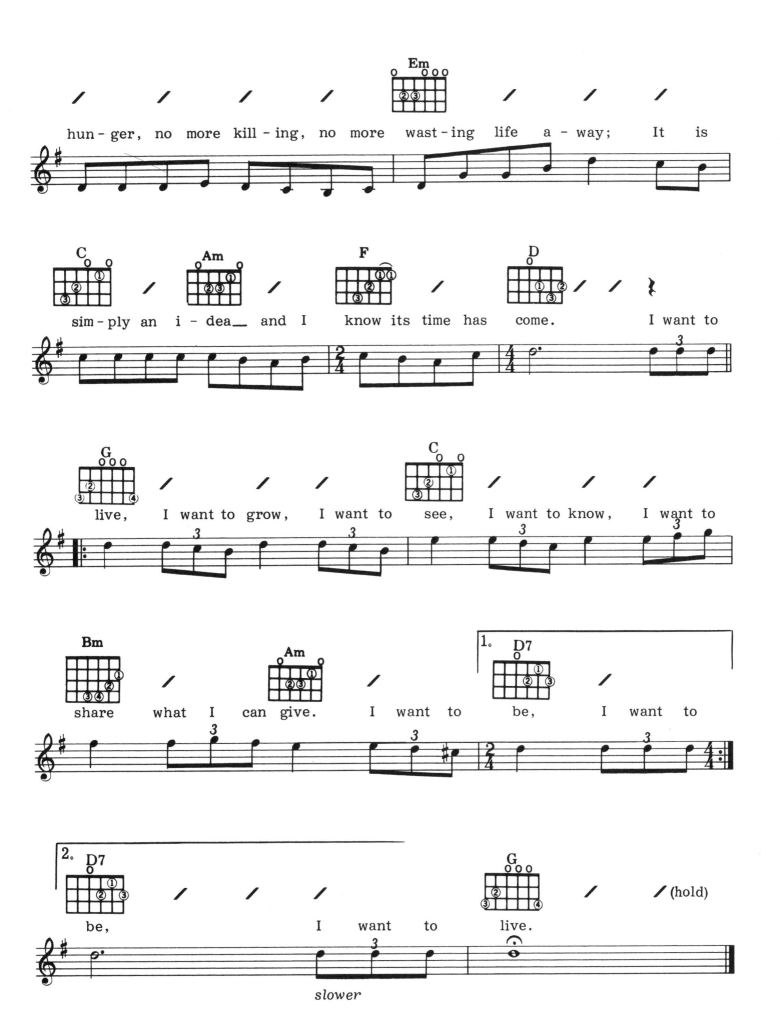

I'd Rather Be A Cowboy (Lady's Chains)

Words and Music by John Denver

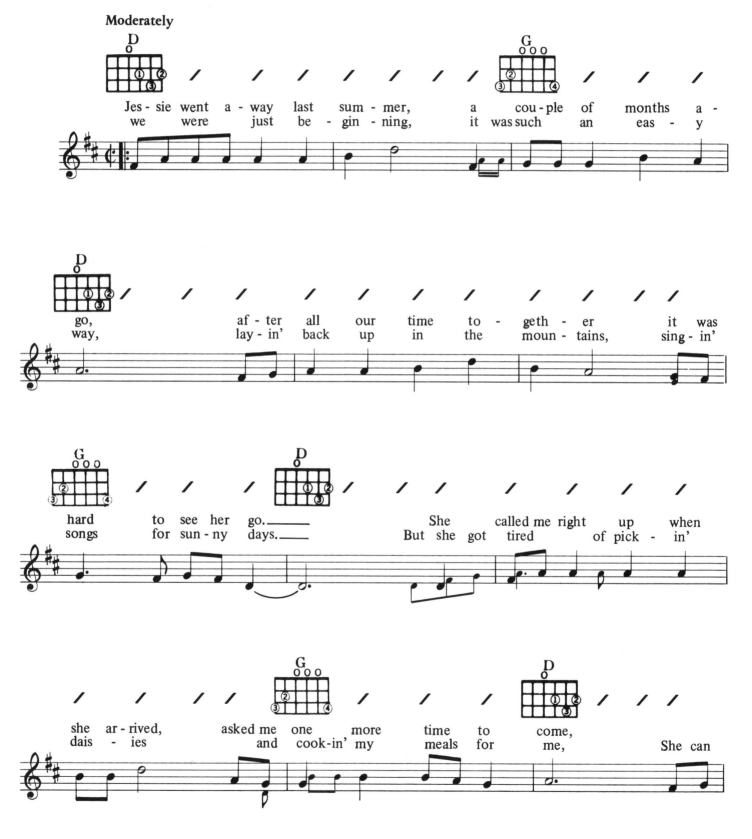

love and la - dy's chains. _____ When _

I'd rath - er live on the side of a moun - tain than

wan - der through can - yons of con - crete _ and steel.

I'd rath - er laugh with the rain _____ and sun -

shine and lay down my sun - down in some star - ry

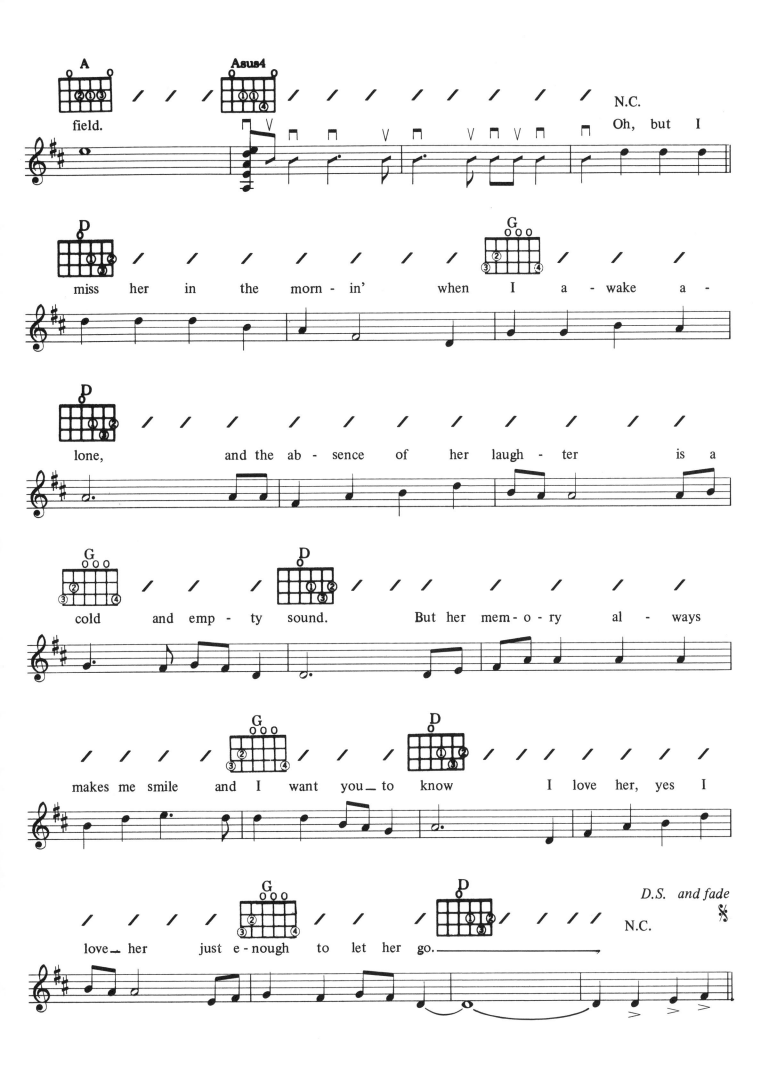

I'm Sorry

Words and Music by John Denver

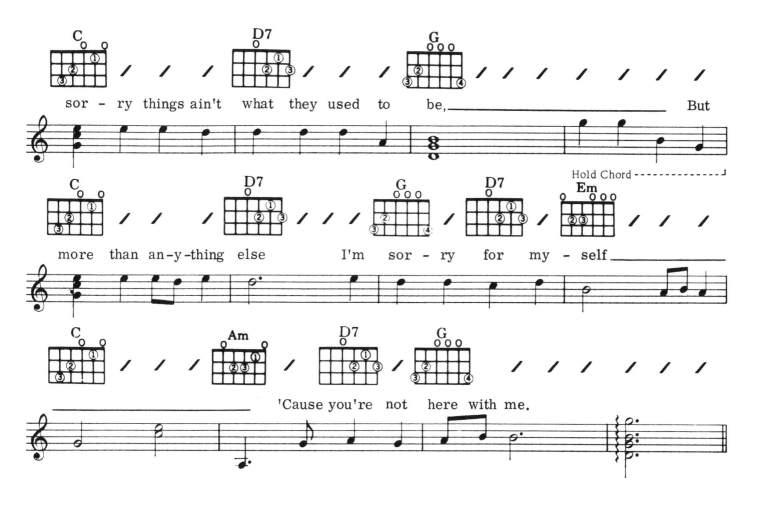

sor - ry things ain't what they used to be,_____ But

more than an-y-thing else I'm sor - ry for my - self_____

'Cause you're not here with me.

(Verse) Our friends all ask about you, I say you're doin' fine
I expect to hear from you almost anytime.
But they all know I'm cryin', that I can't sleep at night,
They all know I'm dyin' down deep inside.

(Chorus) I'm sorry for all the lies I told you,
I'm sorry for the things I didn't say,
But more than anything else I'm sorry for myself
I can't believe you went away.

(Chorus) I'm sorry if I took some things for granted,
I'm sorry for the chains I put on you,
But more than anything else I'm sorry for myself
For livin' without you.
(To Instrumental ending)

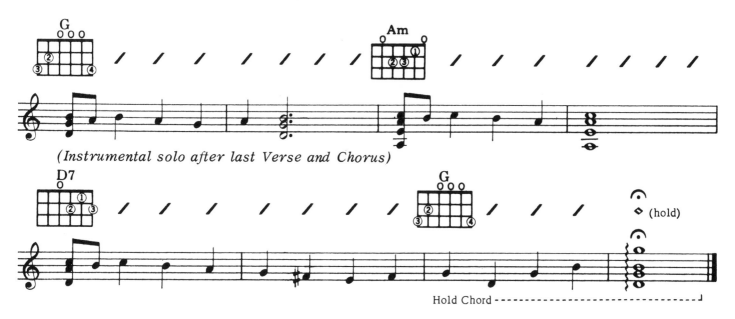

(Instrumental solo after last Verse and Chorus)

Hold Chord -

Joseph & Joe

Words and Music by John Denver

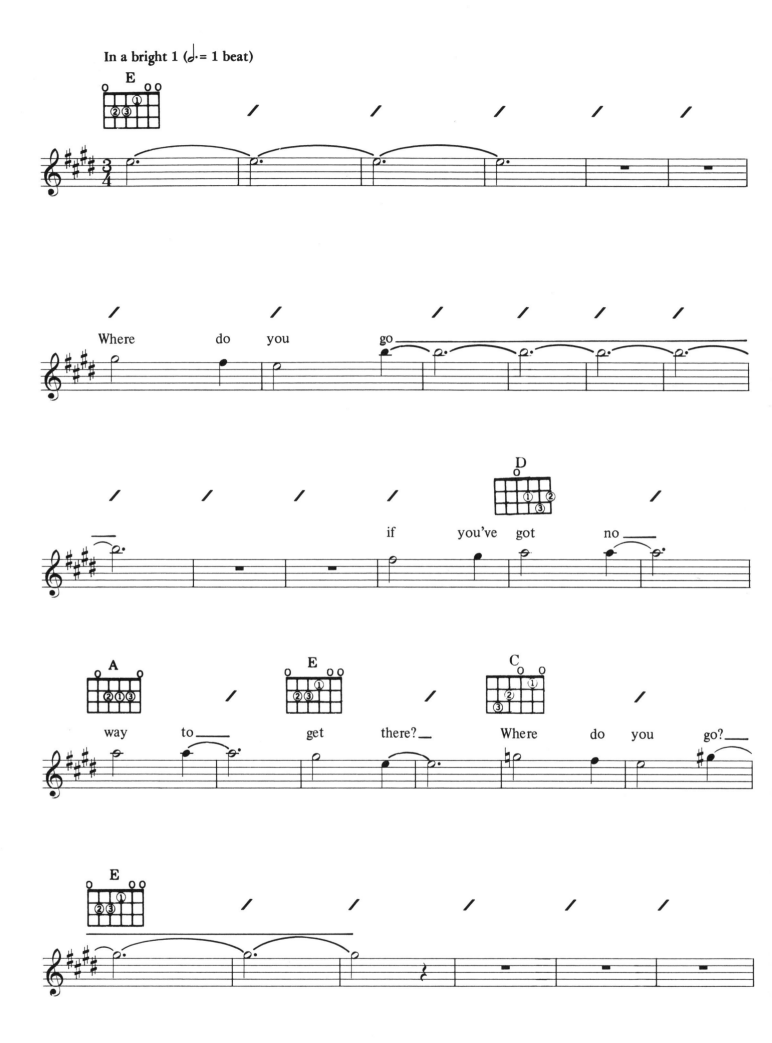

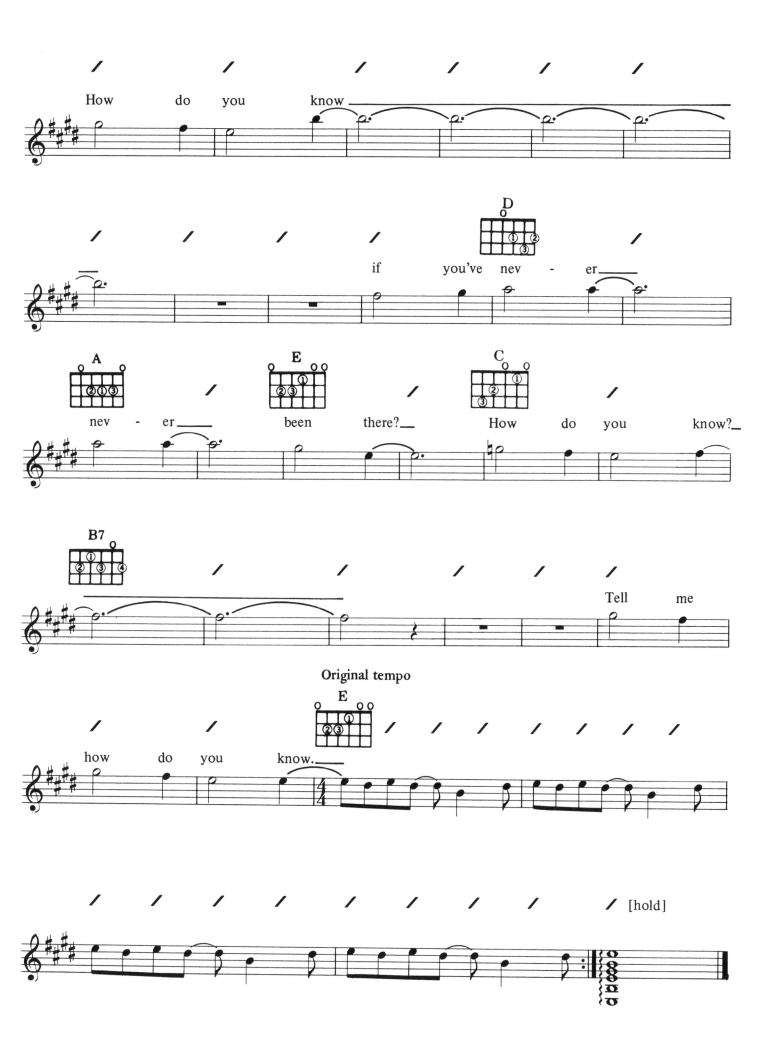

Leaving On A Jet Plane

Words and Music by John Denver

Chorus

71

Looking For Space

Words and Music by John Denver

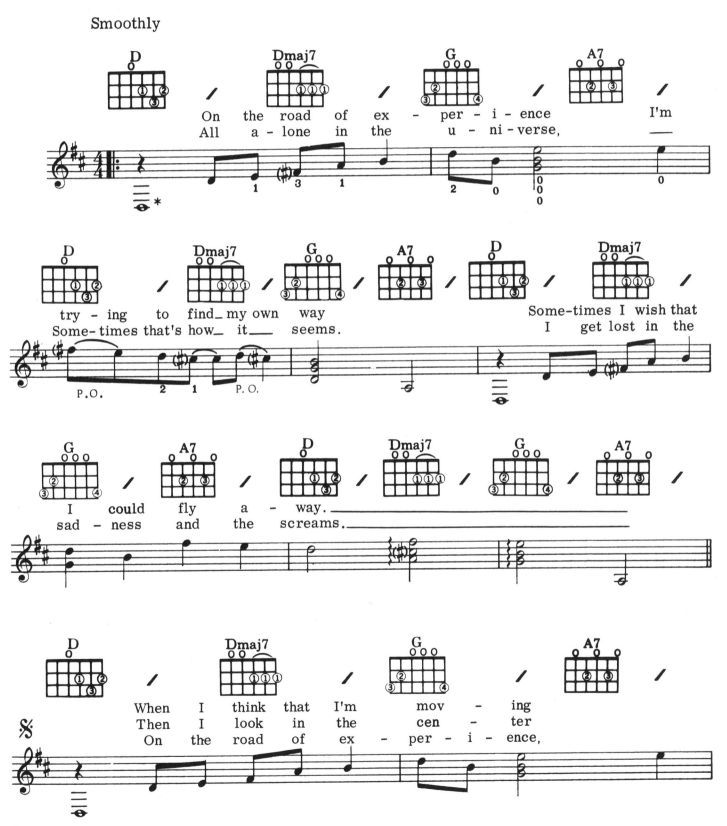

*Tune lowest string to D

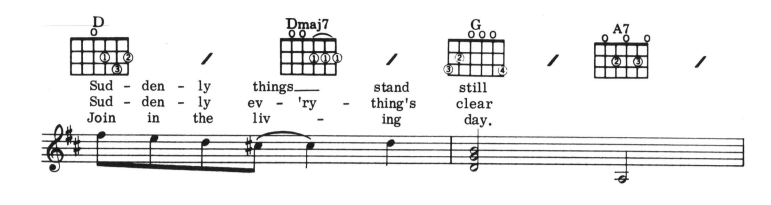

Sud - den - ly things_____ stand still
Sud - den - ly ev - 'ry - thing's clear
Join in the liv - ing day.

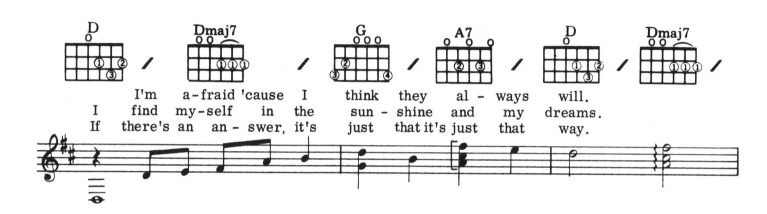

I'm a-fraid 'cause I think they al - ways will.
I find my-self in the sun - shine and my dreams.
If there's an an - swer, it's just that it's just that way.

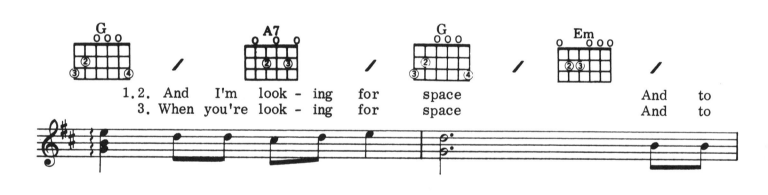

1.2. And I'm look - ing for space And to
3. When you're look - ing for space And to

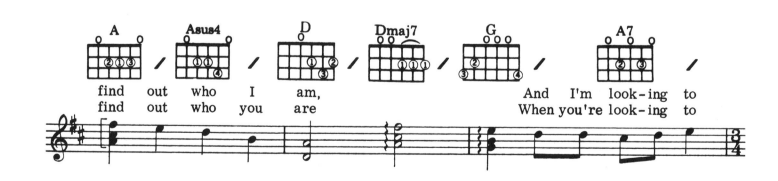

find out who I am, And I'm look-ing to
find out who you are When you're look-ing to

74

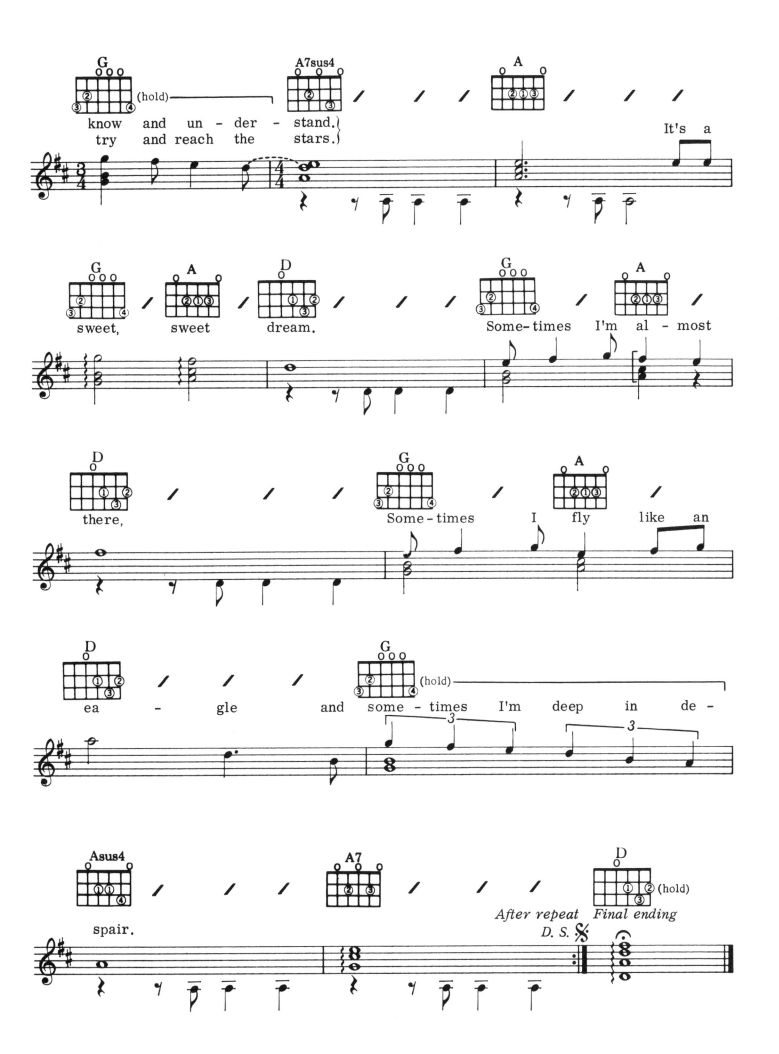

Like A Sad Song

Words and Music by John Denver

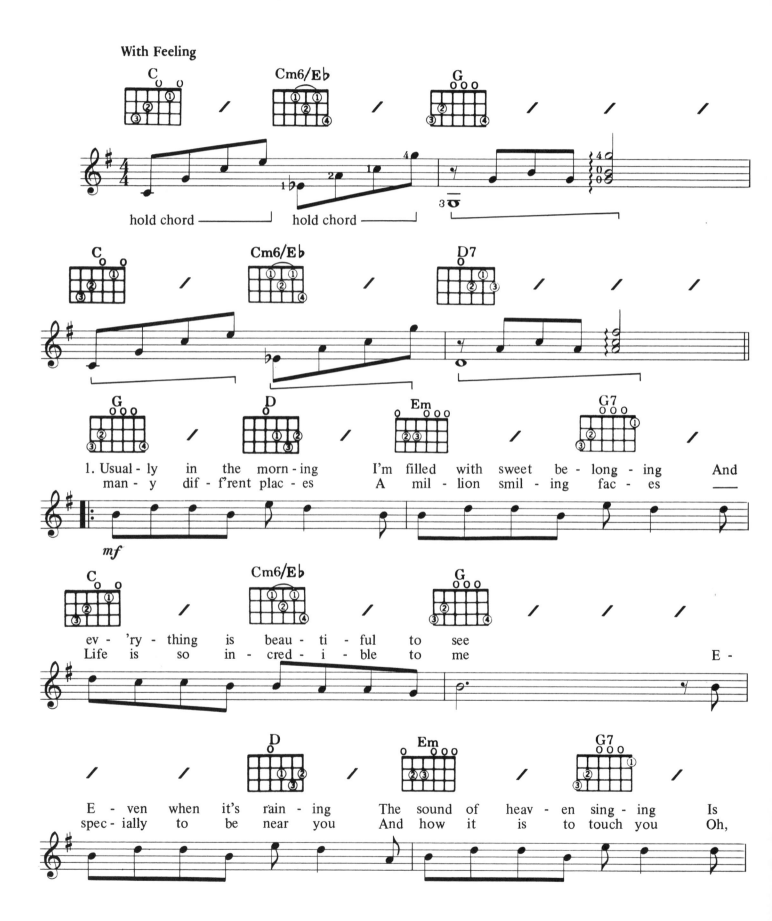

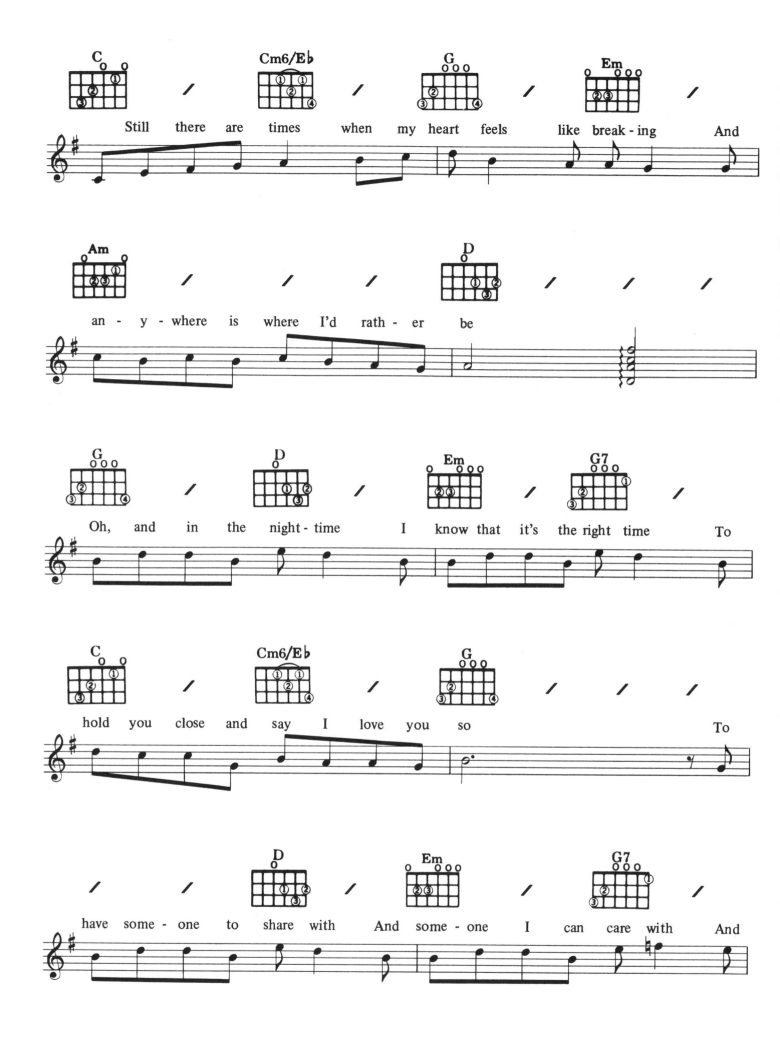

Still there are times when my heart feels like break - ing And

an - y - where is where I'd rath - er be

Oh, and in the night - time I know that it's the right time To

hold you close and say I love you so To

have some - one to share with And some - one I can care with And

Let Us Begin (What Are We Making Weapons For?)

Words and Music by John Denver

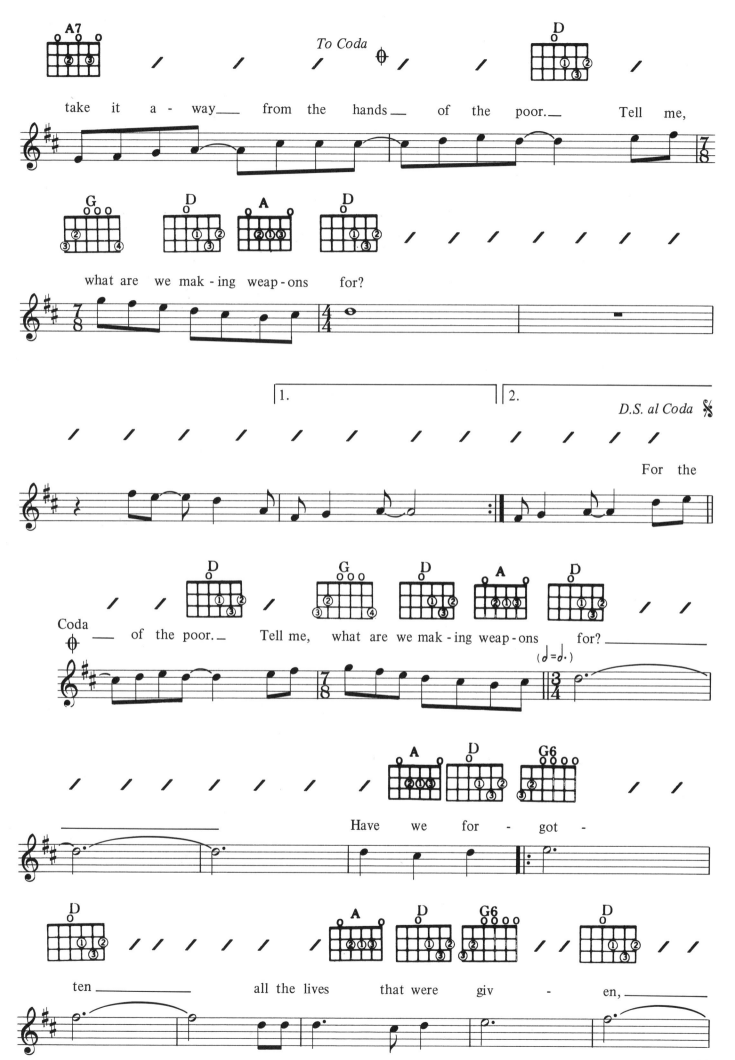

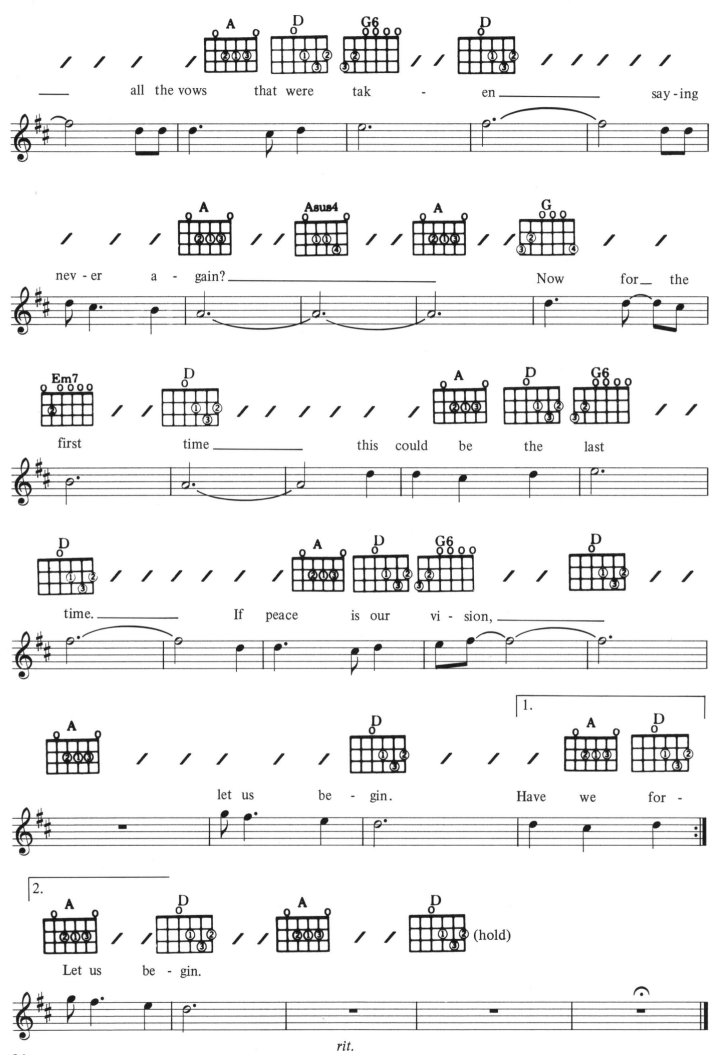

all the vows that were tak - en _____ say-ing

nev - er a - gain? _____ Now for_ the

first time _____ this could be the last

time. _____ If peace is our vi - sion, _____

let us be - gin. Have we for -

Let us be - gin. (hold)

rit.

Never A Doubt

Words and Music by John Denver

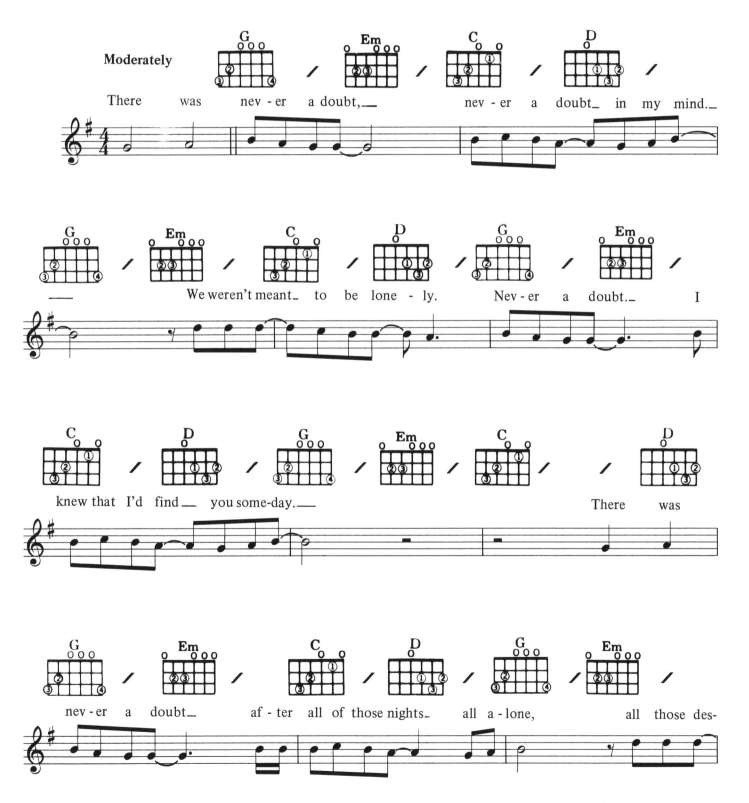

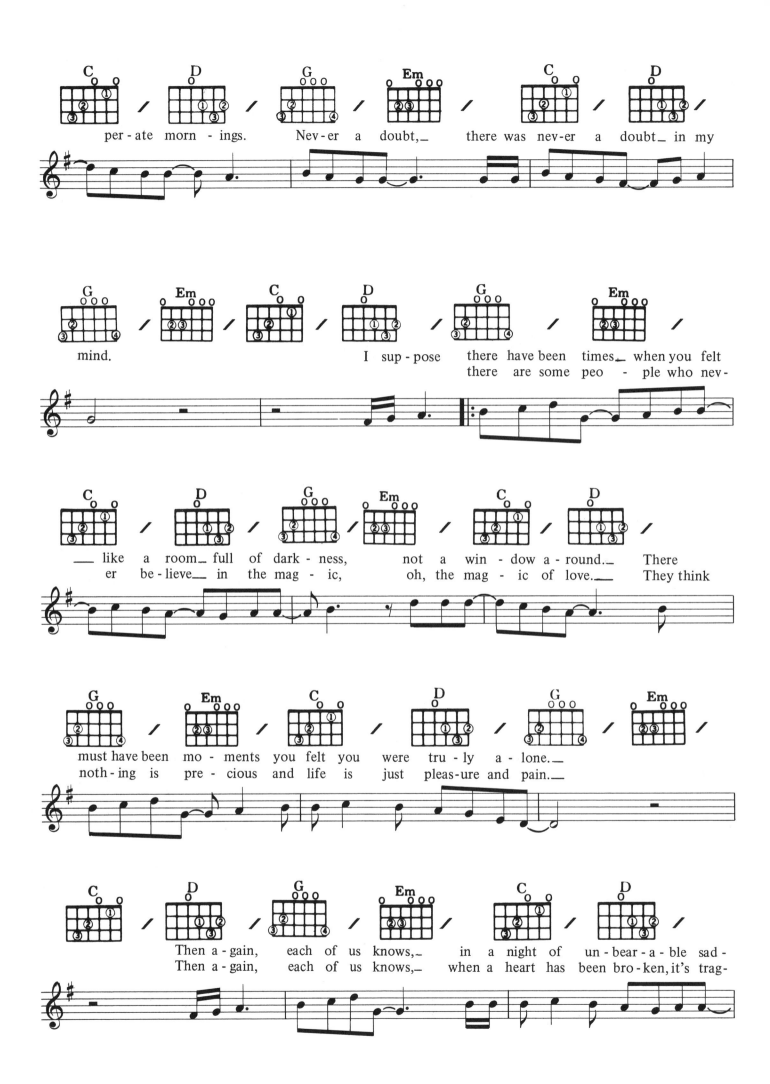

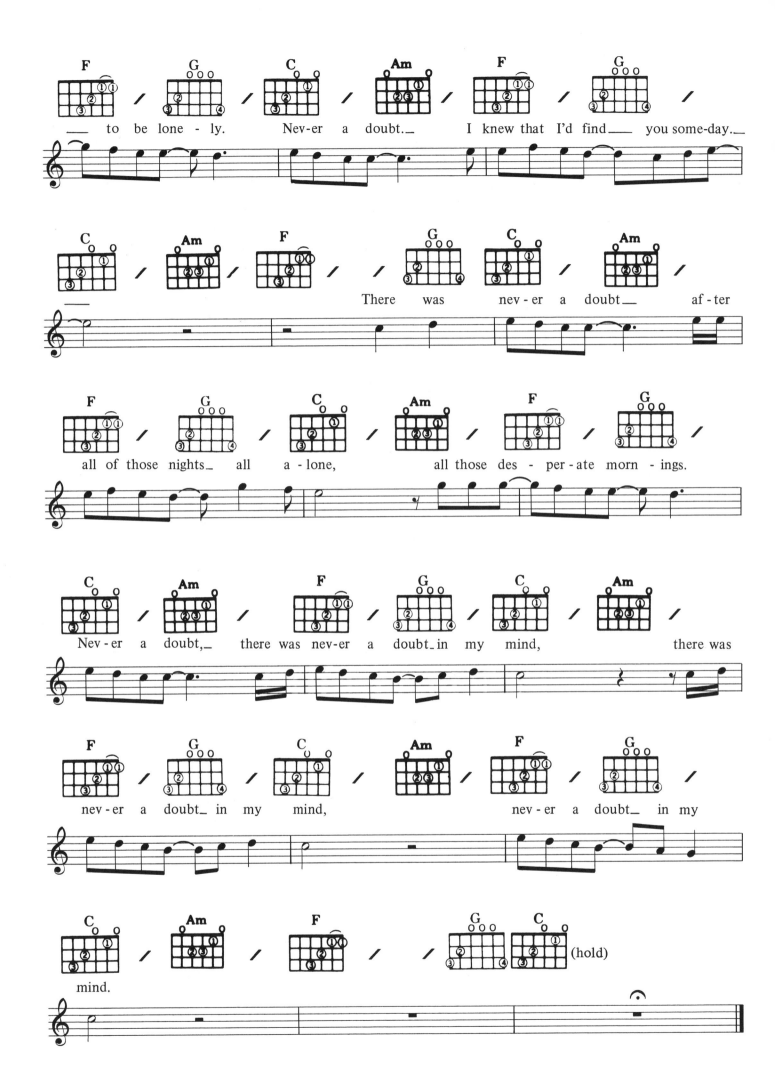

to be lone - ly. Nev-er a doubt.__ I knew that I'd find__ you some-day.__

There was nev - er a doubt__ af - ter

all of those nights_ all a - lone, all those des - per - ate morn - ings.

Nev - er a doubt,__ there was nev - er a doubt_ in my mind, there was

nev - er a doubt_ in my mind, nev - er a doubt_ in my

mind.

(hold)

Rhymes And Reasons

Words and Music by John Denver

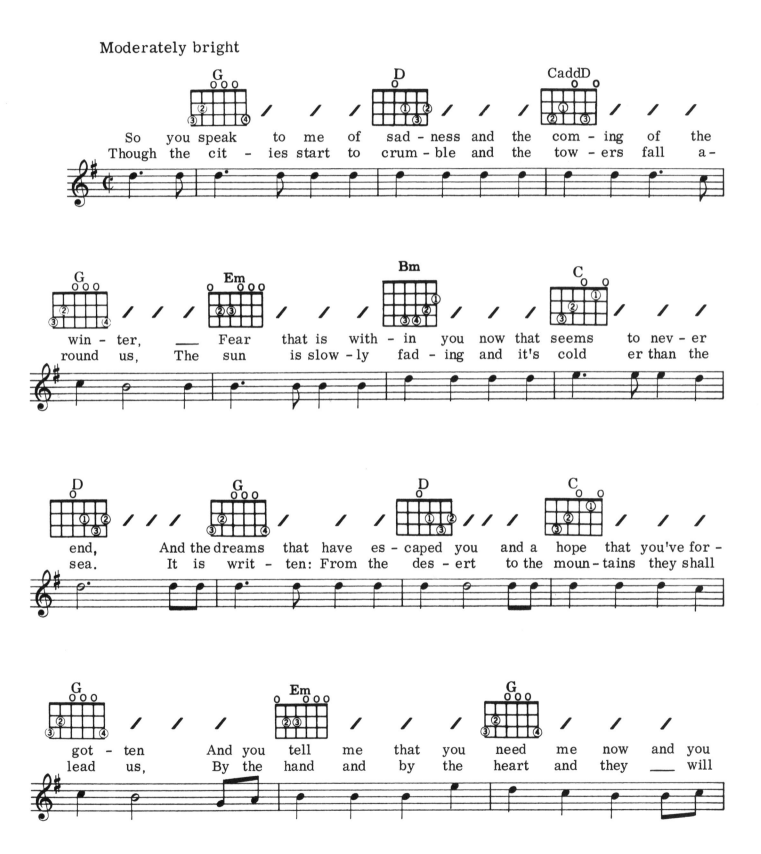

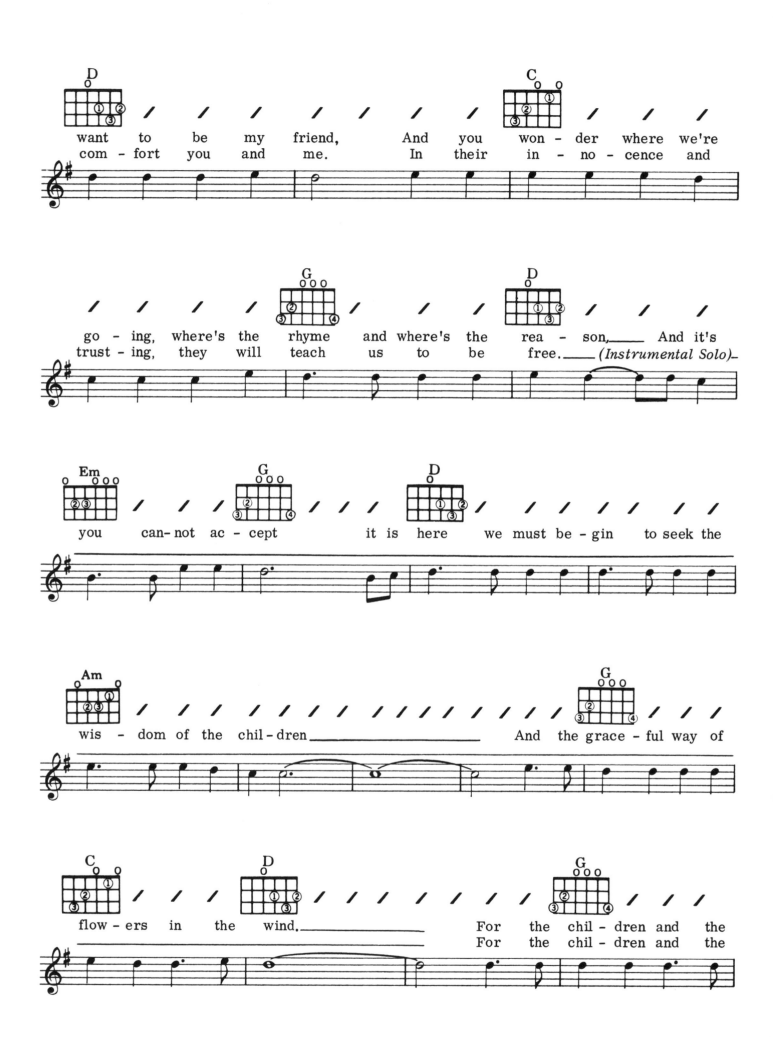

90

Matthew

Words and Music by John Denver

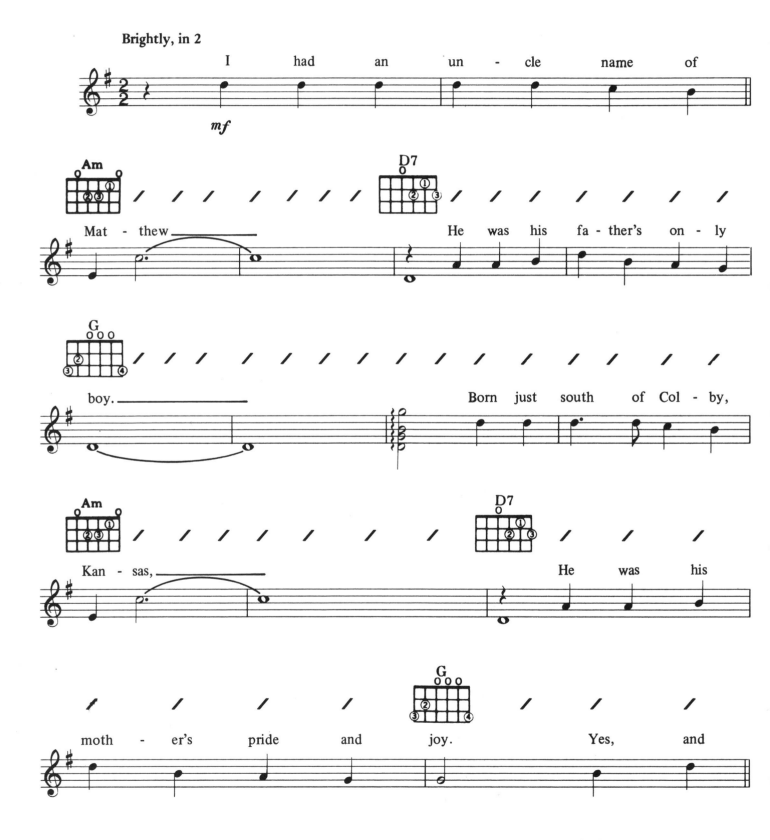

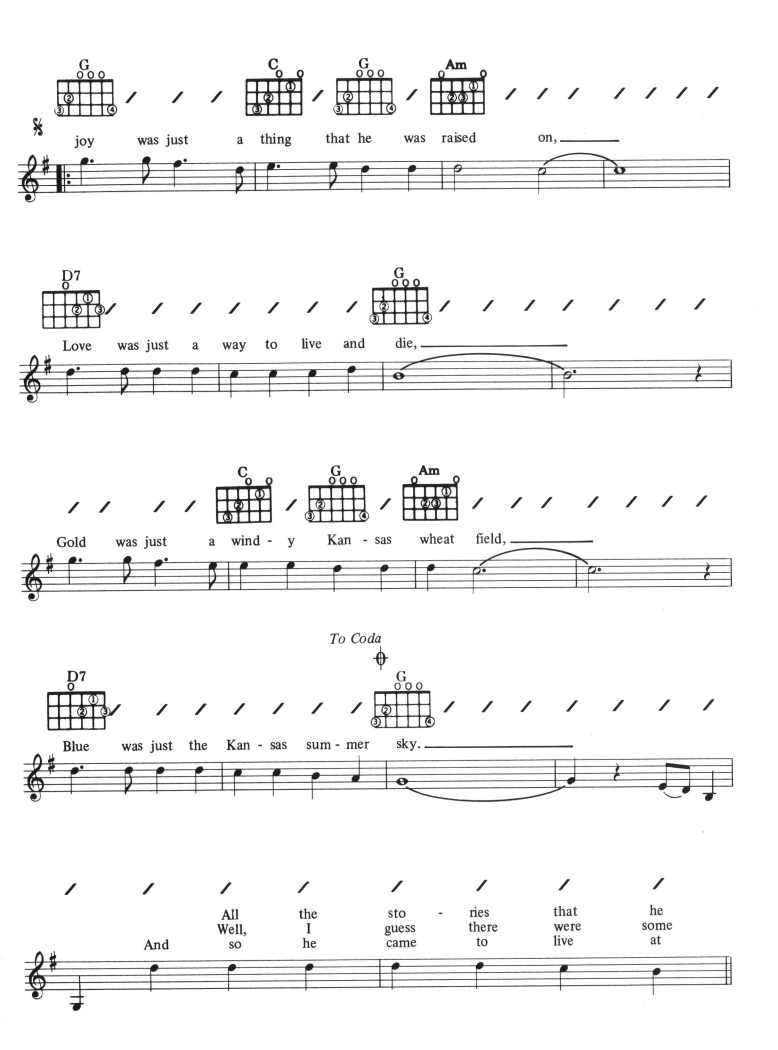

joy was just a thing that he was raised on, _____

Love was just a way to live and die, _____

Gold was just a wind - y Kan - sas wheat field, _____

To Coda

Blue was just the Kan - sas sum - mer sky. _____

All the sto - ries that he
Well, I guess there were some
And so he came to live at

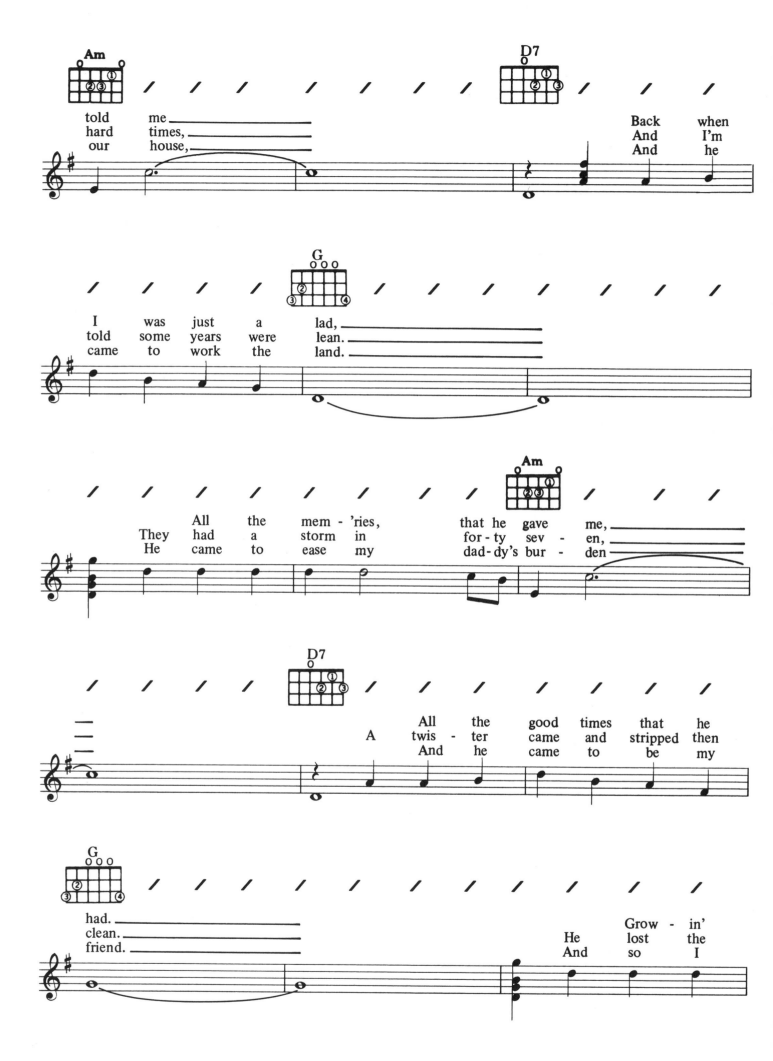

94

My Sweet Lady

Words and Music by John Denver

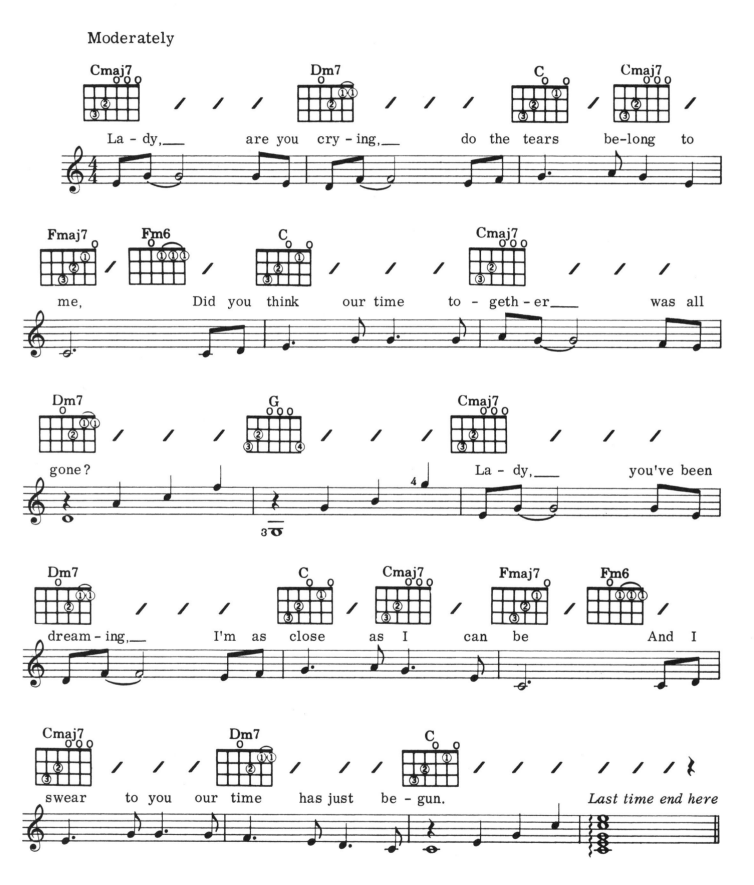

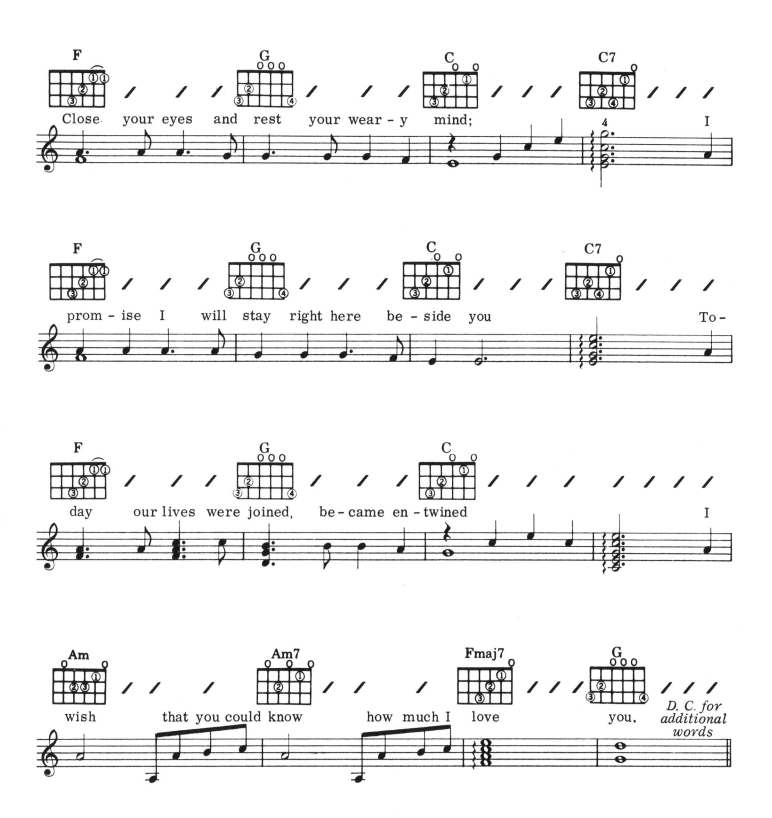

2. Lady, are you happy, do you feel the way I do,
   Are there meanings that you've never seen before?
   Lady, my sweet lady, I just can't believe it's true
   And it's like I've never ever loved before.

   Close your eyes, *(etc.)*

3. *(same as 1st Verse)*

Perhaps Love

Words and Music by John Denver

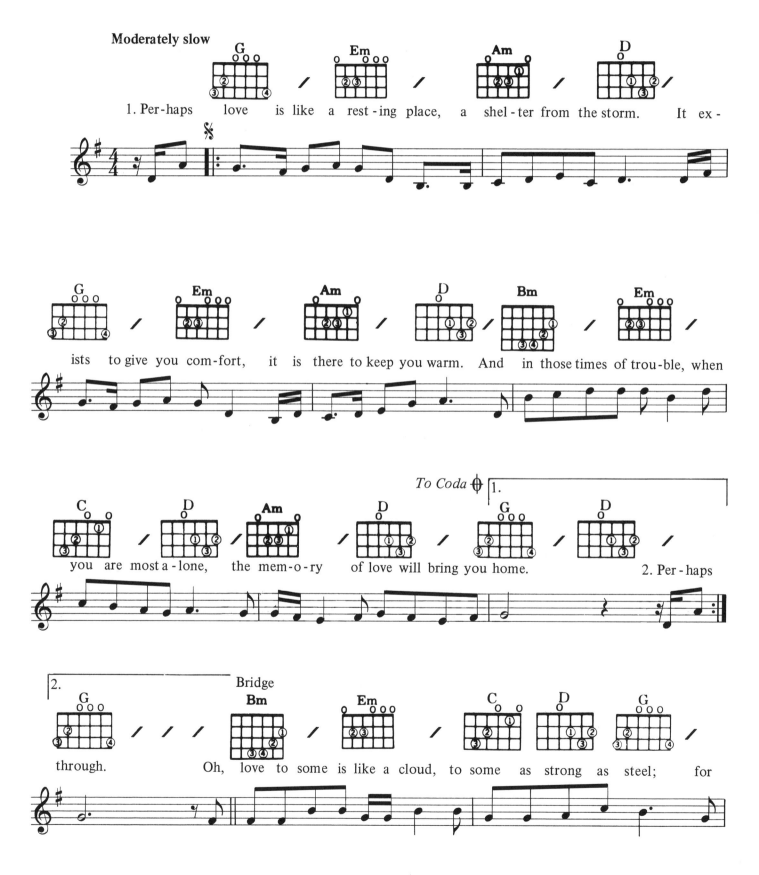

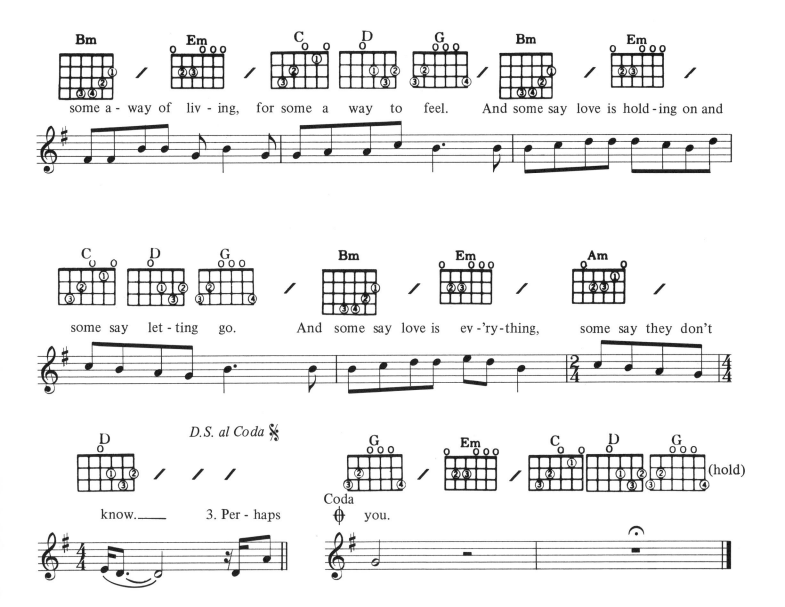

some a - way of liv - ing, for some a way to feel. And some say love is hold - ing on and

some say let - ting go. And some say love is ev -'ry-thing, some say they don't

D.S. al Coda 𝄋

know.___ 3. Per - haps

Coda 𝄌 you.

(hold)

2. Perhaps love is like a window, perhaps an open door.
It invites you to come closer, it wants to show you more.
And even if you lose yourself and don't know what to do,
The memory of love will see you through. *(To Bridge)*

3. Perhaps love is like the ocean, full of conflict, full of pain,
Like a fire when it's cold outside, thunder when it rains.
If you should live forever and all my dreams come true,
My memories of love will be of you.

Poems, Prayers And Promises

Words and Music by John Denver

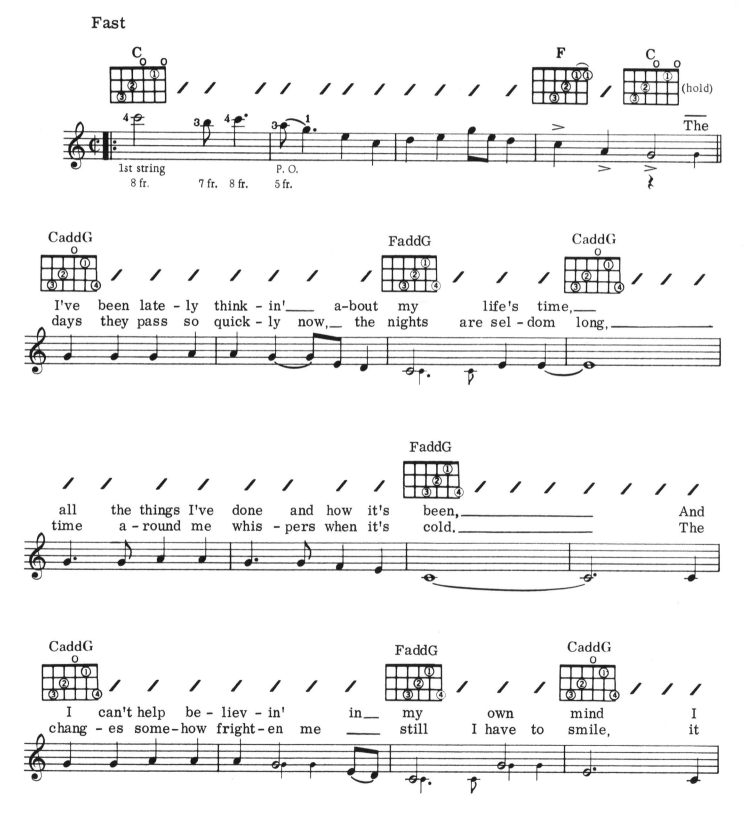

FaddG

/ / / / / / / / / / / / / / / /

know   I'm gon - na   hate   to see   it   end._____   I've
turns   me on to   think of grow - ing old._____   For

CaddG   FaddG   CaddG

/ / / / / / / / / / / / / / /

seen   a lot   of sun - shine,_____   slept   out   in the   rain,   _
tho'   my life's been good to me, there's still   so much to   do,   so

FaddG

/ / / / / / / / / / / / / / / /

spent   a night or   two   all on my   own,_____   I've
man - y things my mind has nev - er   known,_____   I'd

CaddG   FaddG   CaddG

/ / / / / / / / / / / / / / /

known   my la - dy's pleas - ures,   _   had   my-self some friends,
like   to raise a   fam - 'ly,   I'd   like   to sail a - way,   and

FaddG

/ / / / / / / / / / / / / / / /

spent   a time or   two   in my own   home._____   I
dance   a-cross the   moun - tains on   the   moon._____   I

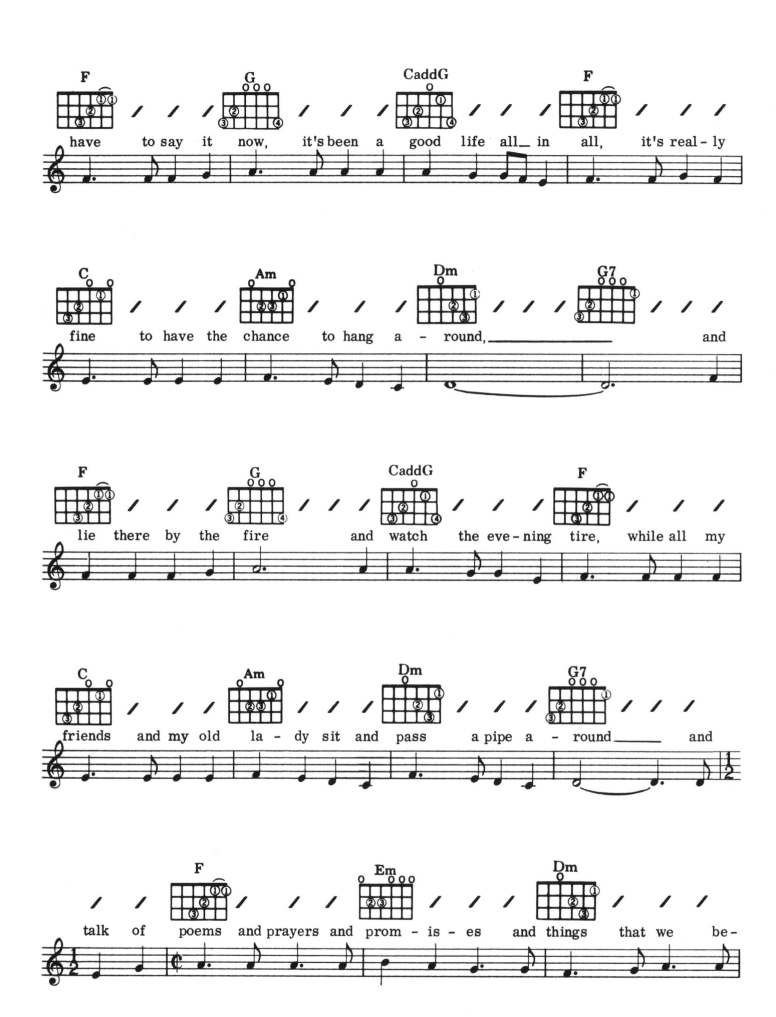

Rocky Mountain High

Words by John Denver
Music by John Denver and Mike Taylor

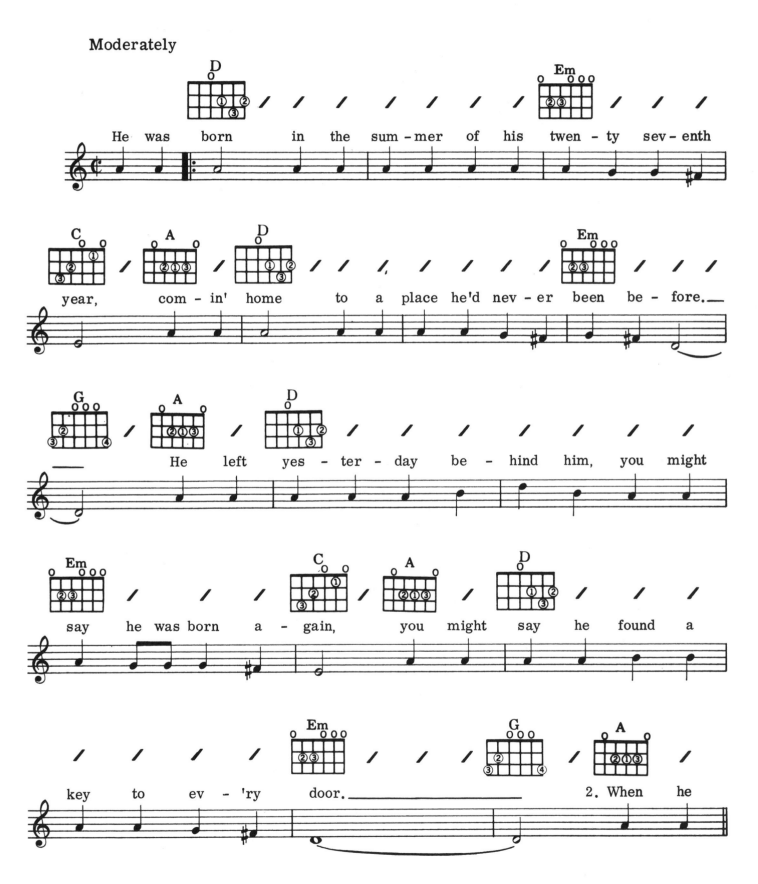

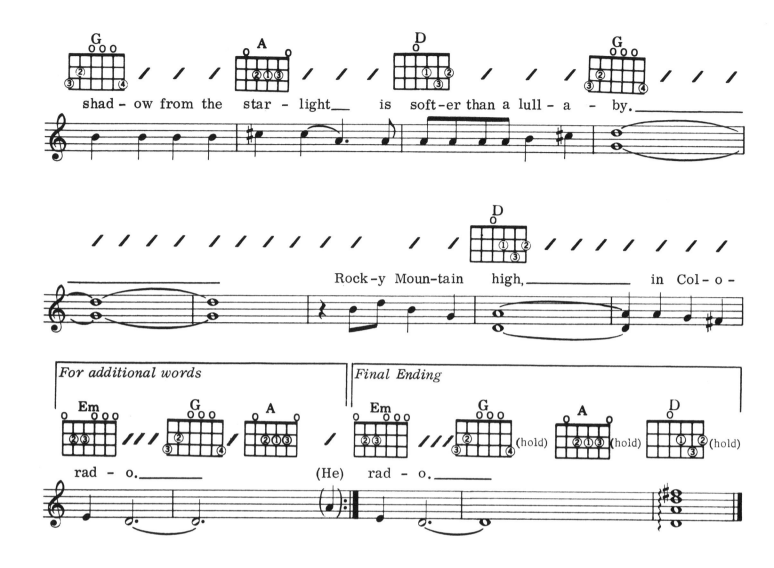

Verse 3. He climbed cathedral mountains, he saw silver clouds below,
He saw everything as far as you can see.
And they say that he got crazy once and he tried to touch the sun,
And he lost a friend but kept his memory.

Verse 4. Now he walks in quiet solitude, the forests and the streams
Seeking grace in every step he takes.
His sight has turned inside himself to try and understand
The serenity of a clear blue mountain lake.

Chorus 2. And the Colorado Rocky Mountain high,
I've seen it rainin' fire in the sky.
Talk to God and listen to the casual reply.
Rocky Mountain high in Colorado.

Verse 5. Now his life is full of wonder, but his heart still knows some fear
Of a simple thing he cannot comprehend.
Why they try to tear the mountains down to bring in a couple more,
More people, more scars upon the land.

Chorus 3. And the Colorado Rocky Mountain high,
I've seen it rainin' fire in the sky.
I know he'd be a poorer man if he never saw an eagle fly.
Rocky Mountain high.
It's a Colorado Rocky Mountain high (etc.)

106

Seasons Of The Heart

Words and Music by John Denver

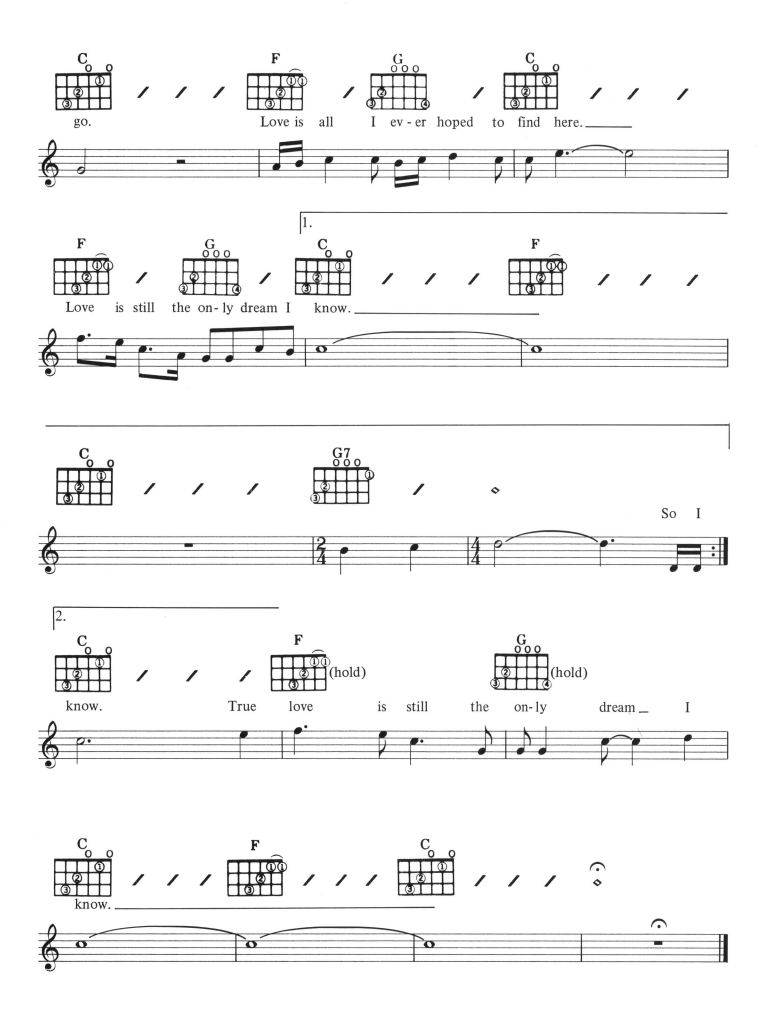

Shanghai Breezes

Words and Music by John Denver

112

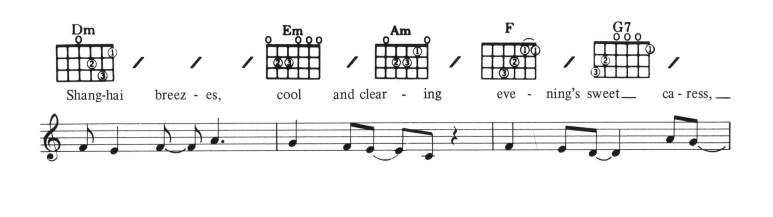

Shang-hai breez - es, cool and clear - ing eve - ning's sweet ca - ress,

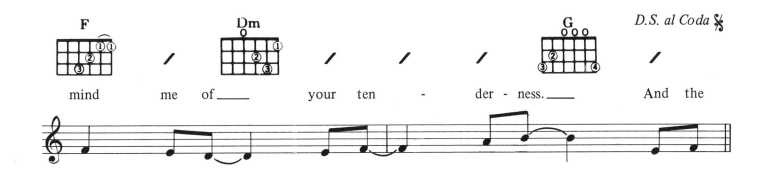

Shang-hai breez - es soft and gen - tle re -

D.S. al Coda 𝄋

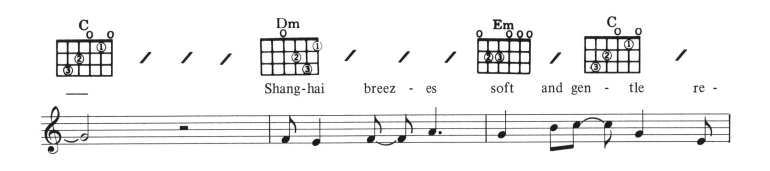

mind me of your ten - der - ness. And the

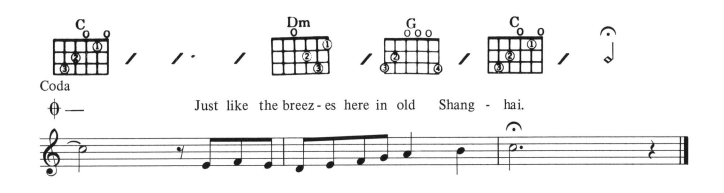

Coda

Just like the breez - es here in old Shang - hai.

Sunshine On My Shoulders

Words by John Denver
Music by John Denver, Mike Taylor and Dick Kniss

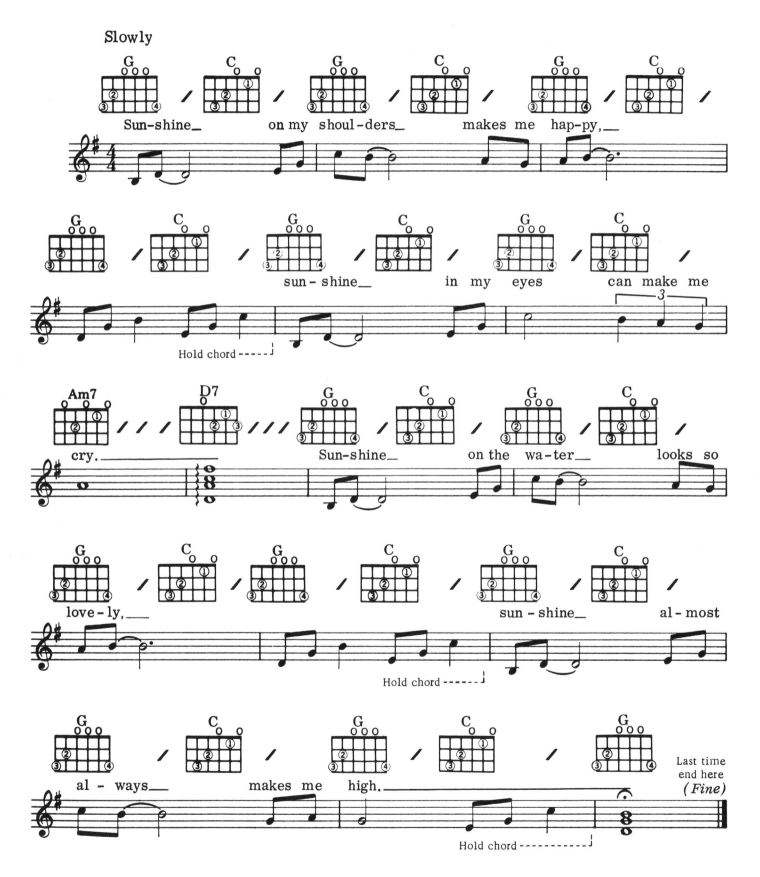

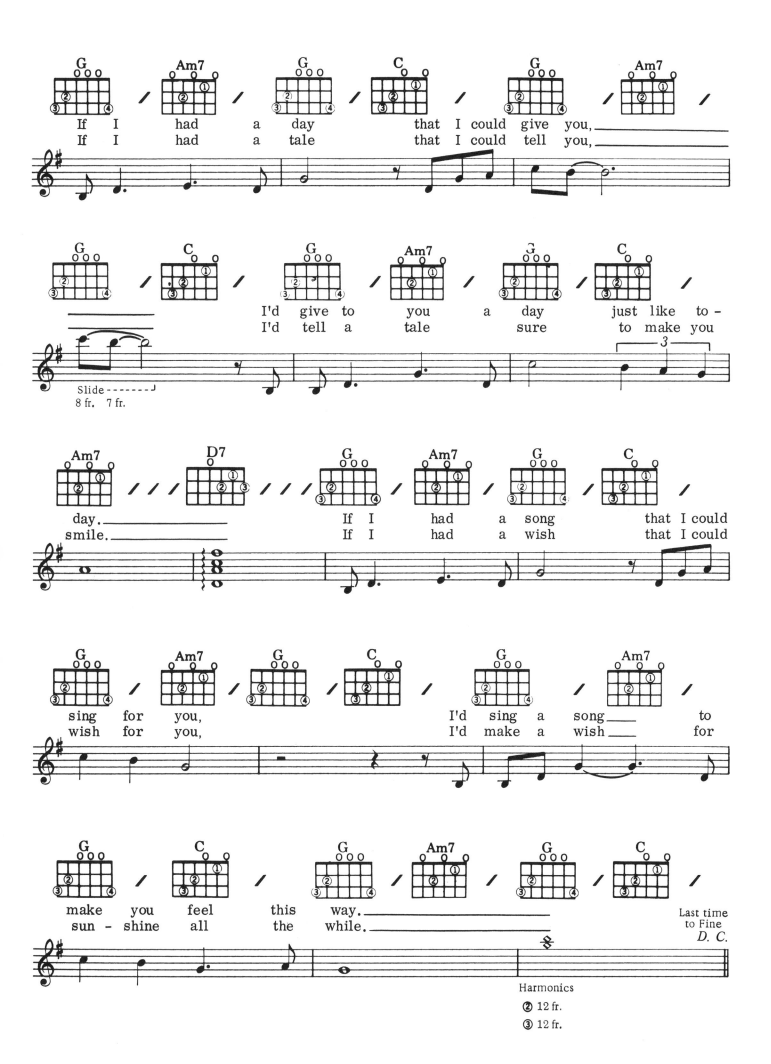

Take Me Home, Country Roads

Words and Music by Bill Danoff, Taffy Nivert and John Denver

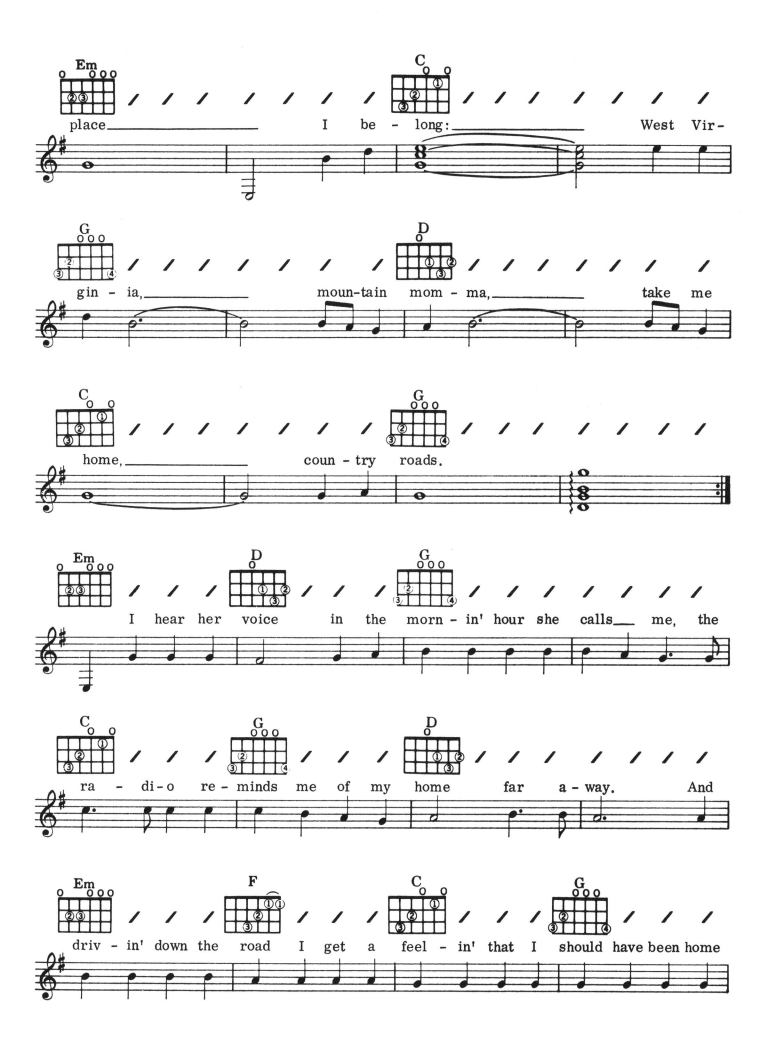

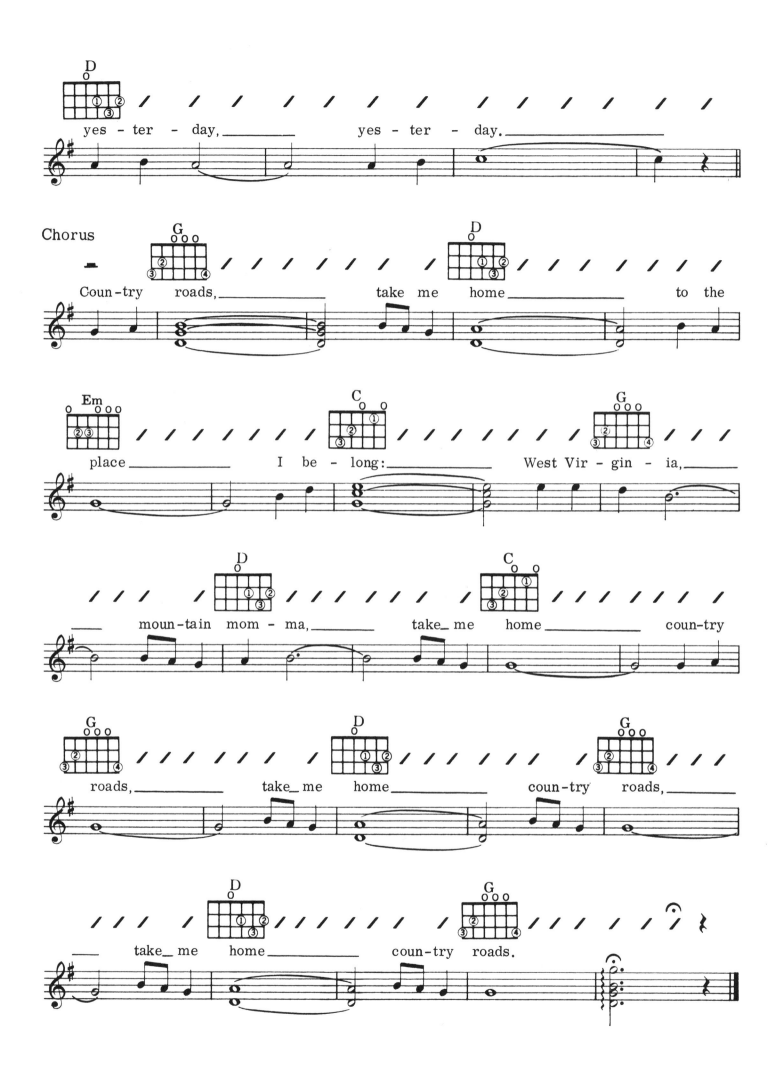

Chorus

yes - ter - day,_____ yes - ter - day._____

Coun-try roads,_____ take me home _____ to the

place _____ I be - long:_____ West Vir - gin - ia,_____

____ moun-tain mom - ma,_____ take_ me home _____ coun-try

roads,_____ take_ me home _____ coun-try roads,_____

____ take_ me home _____ coun-try roads.

To The Wild Country

Words and Music by John Denver

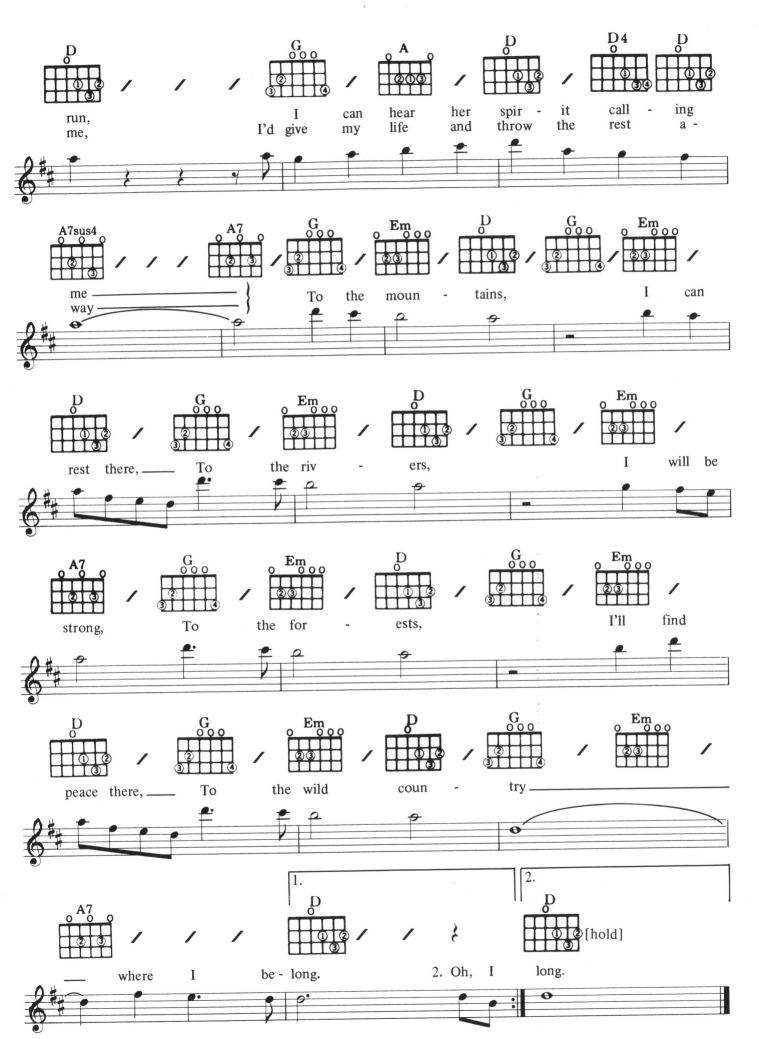

Thank God I'm A Country Boy

Words and Music by John Martin Sommers

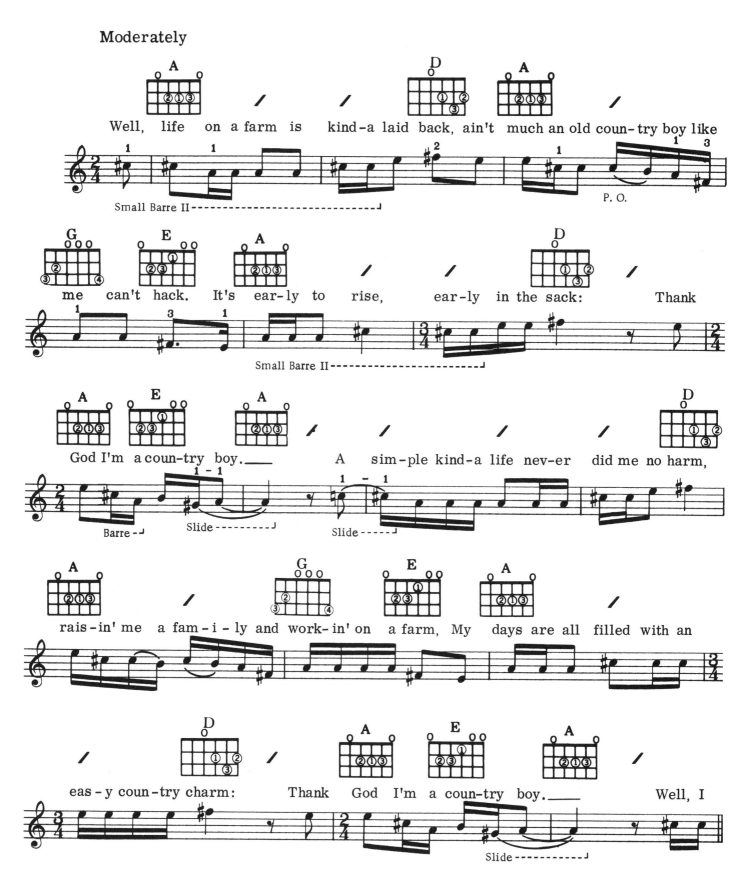

Chorus

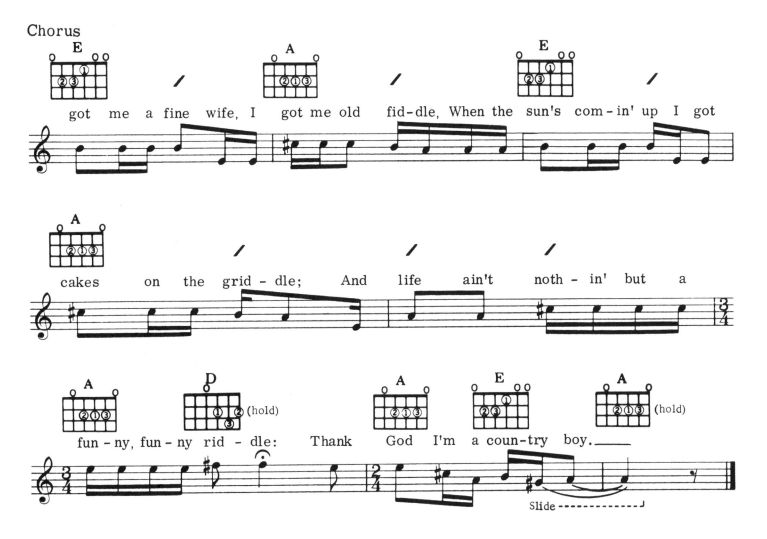

got me a fine wife, I got me old fid-dle, When the sun's com-in' up I got

cakes on the grid-dle; And life ain't noth-in' but a

fun-ny, fun-ny rid-dle: Thank God I'm a coun-try boy.____

Slide - - - - - - - - - - - - ⌐

When the work's all done and the sun's settin' low
I pull out my fiddle and I rosin up the bow.
But the kids are asleep so I keep it kinda low:
Thank God I'm a country boy.
I'd play "Sally Goodin'" all day if I could,
But the Lord and my wife wouldn't take it very good.
So I fiddle when I can and I work when I should:
Thank God I'm a country boy.
(Chorus)

I wouldn't trade my life for diamonds or jewels,
I never was one of them money hungry fools.
I'd rather have my fiddle and my farmin' tools:
Thank God I'm a country boy.
Yeah, city folk drivin' in a black limousine,
A lotta sad people thinkin' that's mighty keen.
Well folks, let me tell you now exactly what I mean:
I thank God I'm a country boy.
(Chorus)

Well, my fiddle was my daddy's till the day he died,
And he took me by the hand and held me close to his side.
He said, "Live a good life and play my fiddle with pride,
And thank God you're a country boy."
My daddy taught me young how to hunt and how to whittle,
He taught me how to work and play a tune on the fiddle.
He taught me how to love and how to give just a little:
Thank God I'm a country boy.
(Chorus)

Welcome To My Morning (Farewell Andromeda)

Words and Music by John Denver

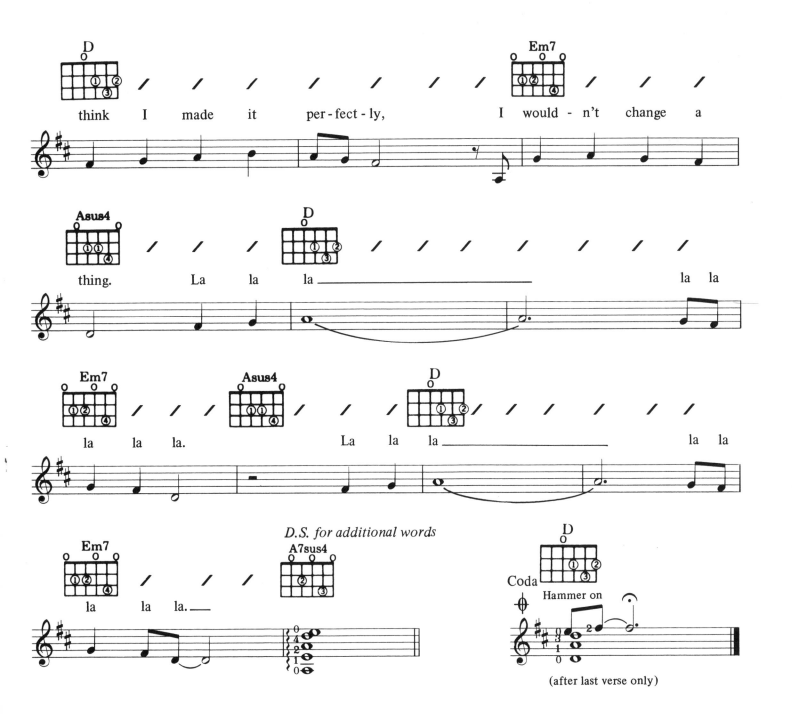

Welcome to my happiness, you know it makes me smile
And it pleases me to have you here for just a little while,
While we open up the spaces and try to break some chains.
And if the truth is told they will never come again.
La la la *etc.*

Welcome to my evenin', the closin' of the day,
You know I could try a million times, never find a better way
To tell you that I love you and all the songs I played
Are to thank you for allowing me in the lovely day you made.

Welcome to my mornin', welcome to my day,
Oh, yes, I'm the only one responsible, I made it just this way
To make myself some pictures and see what they might bring.
I think I made it perfectly, I wouldn't change a thing.
La la la *etc.*

Whispering Jesse

Words and Music by John Denver

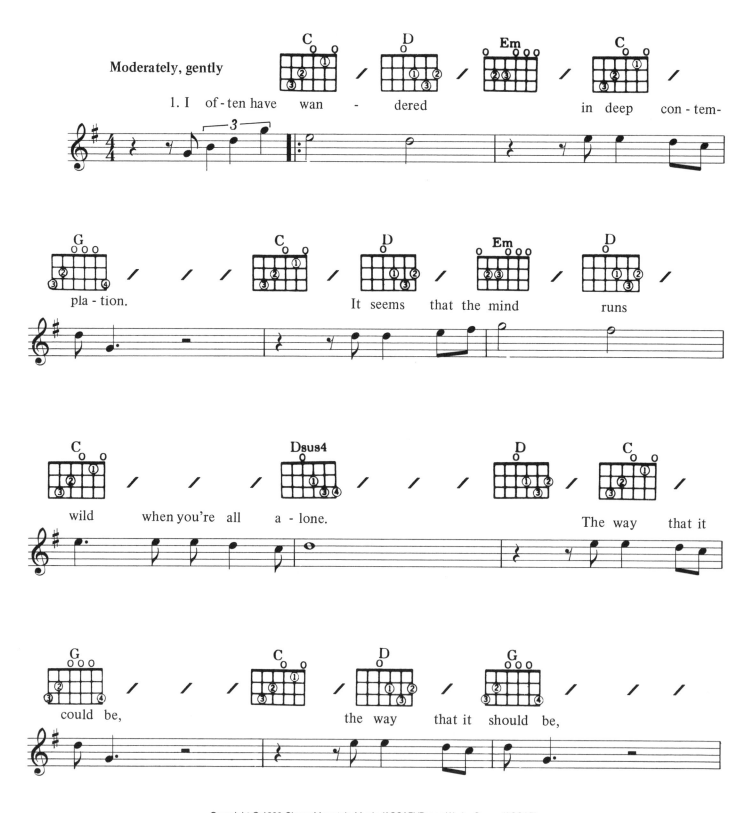

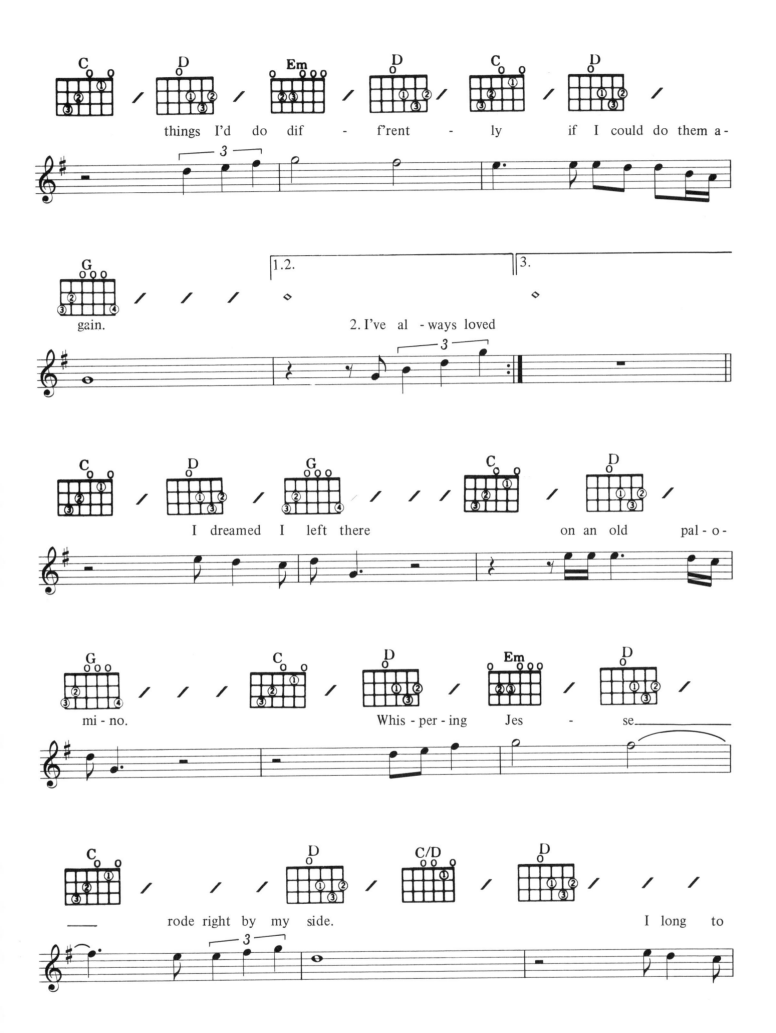

hold her,   to hear   her soft breath - ing,

the touch of   her   cool   hands_____   on my   fe - vered

brow.

1.2.

3.

(hold)
Whis - per - ing   Jes   -   se   still rides   in the

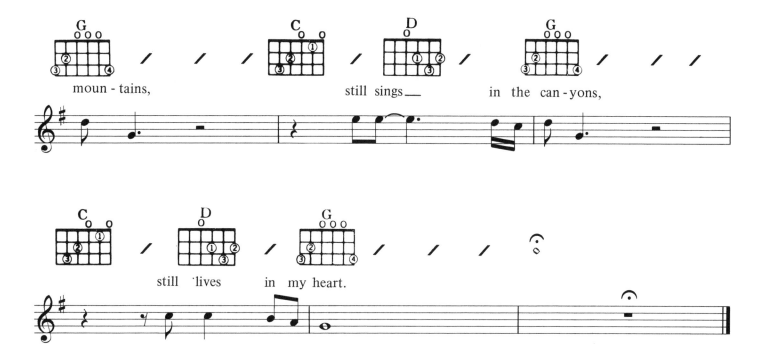

moun - tains, still sings___ in the can - yons,

still lives in my heart.

2. I've always loved springtime, the passing of winter,
   The green of the new leaves and life goin' on.
   The promise of morning, the long days of summer,
   Warm nights of loving her beneath the bright stars.

3. I'm just an old cowboy from high Colorado,
   Too old to ride anymore, too blind to see.
   I sleep in the city now, away from my mountains,
   Away from the cabin we always called home.

Wild Montana Skies

Words and Music by John Denver

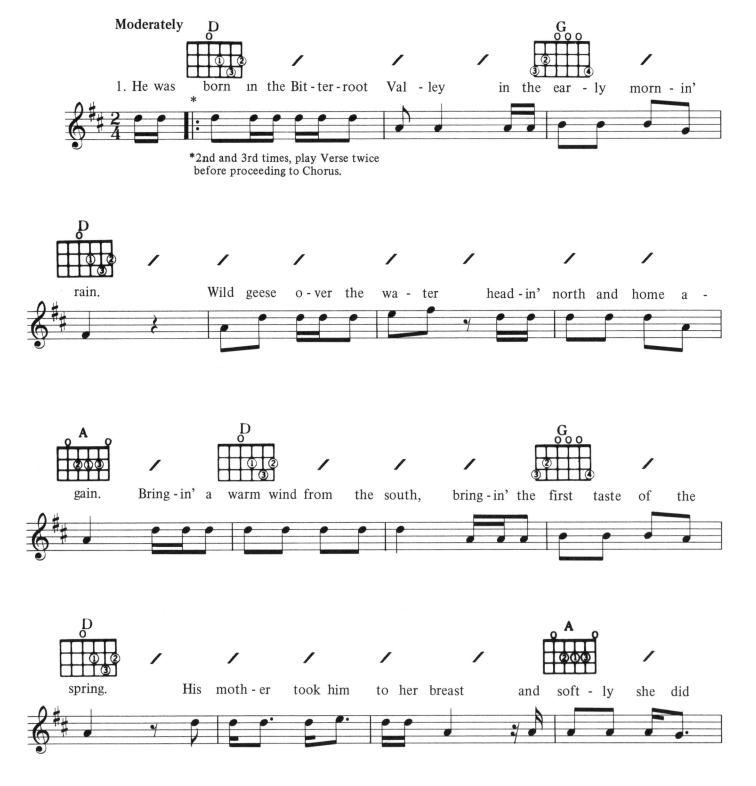

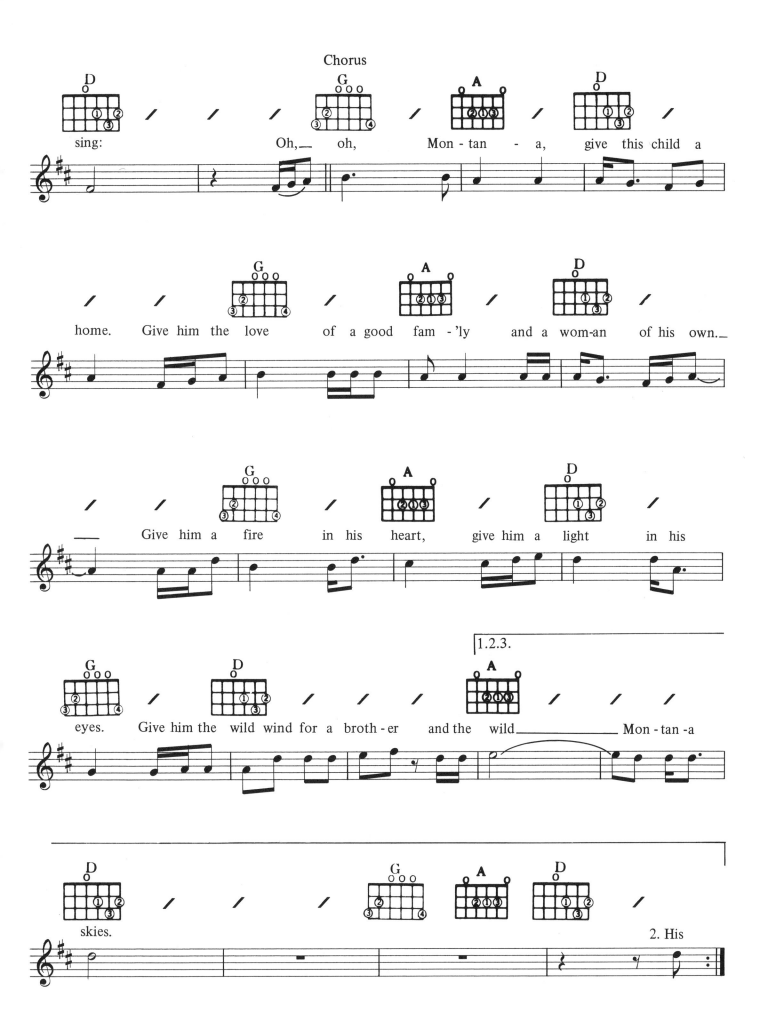

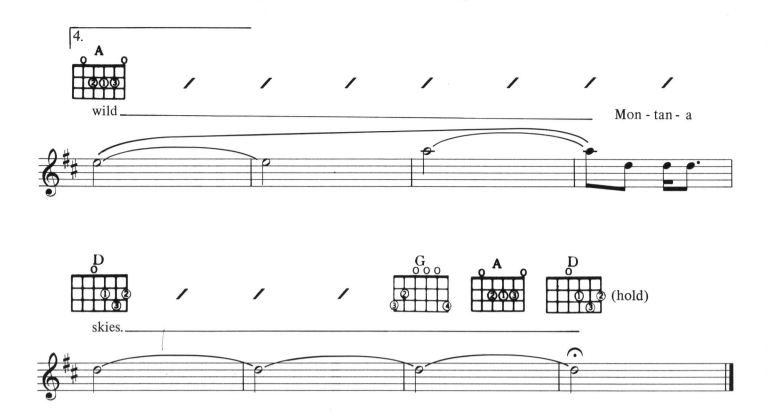

wild _____ Mon - tan - a

skies. _____ (hold)

2. His mother died that summer, he never learned to cry.
   He never knew his father, he never did ask why.
   And he never knew the answers that would make an easy way.
   But he learned to know the wilderness and to be a man that way.

3. His mother's brother took him in to his family and his home,
   Gave him a hand that he could lean on and a strength to call his own.
   And he learned to be a farmer, and he learned to love the land,
   And he learned to read the seasons, and he learned to make a stand. *(To Chorus)*

4. On the eve of his twenty-first birthday he set out on his own.
   He was thirty years and runnin' when he found his way back home.
   Ridin' a storm across the mountains and an achin' in his heart,
   Said he came to turn the pages and to make a brand-new start.

5. Now, he never told the story of the time that he was gone.
   Some say he was a lawyer, some say he was a john.
   There was somethin' in the city that he said he couldn't breathe,
   And there was somethin' in the country that he said he couldn't leave. *(To Chorus)*

6. Now, some say he was crazy, some are glad he's gone.
   But some of us will miss him and we'll try to carry on.
   Giving a voice to the forest, giving a voice to the dawn,
   Giving a voice to the wilderness and the land that he lived on. *(To Chorus)*

How Can I Leave You Again

Words and Music by John Denver

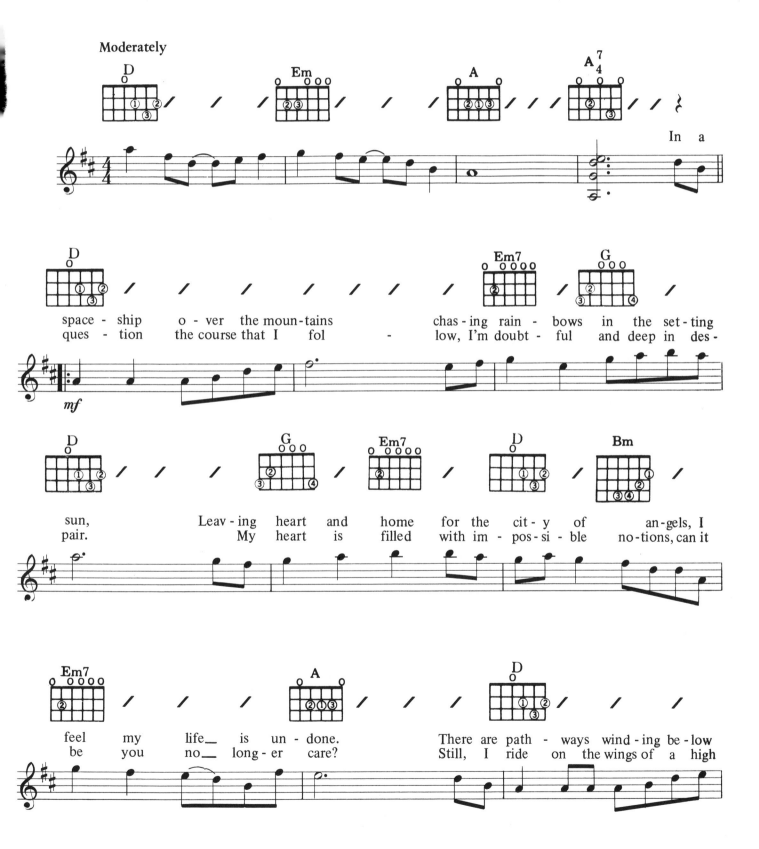

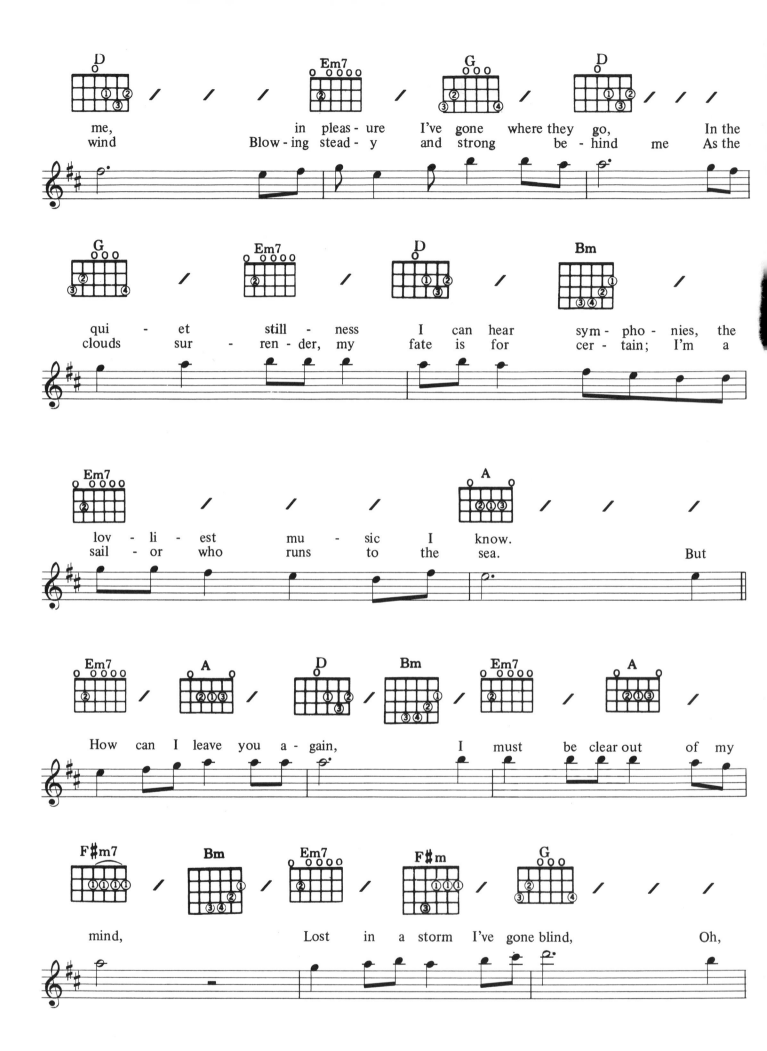

me,
in pleas - ure I've gone where they go, In the
wind Blow - ing stead - y and strong be - hind me As the

qui - et still - ness I can hear sym - pho - nies, the
clouds sur - ren - der, my fate is for cer - tain; I'm a

lov - li - est mu - sic I know.
sail - or who runs to the sea. But

How can I leave you a - gain, I must be clear out of my

mind, Lost in a storm I've gone blind, Oh,

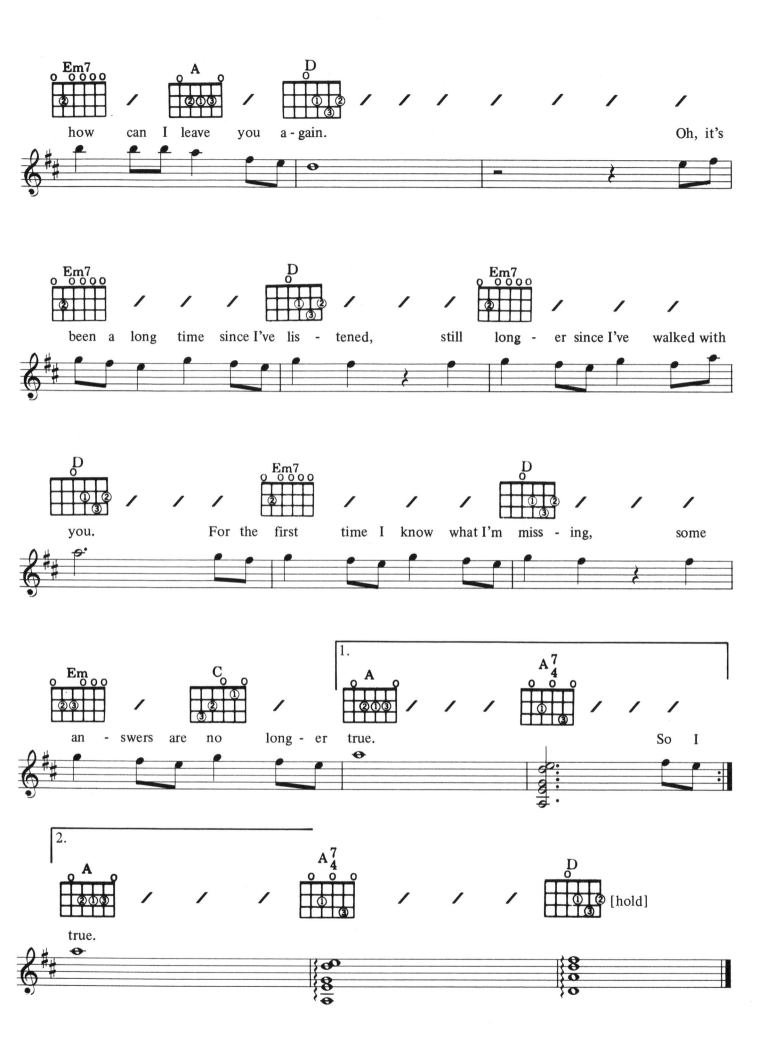

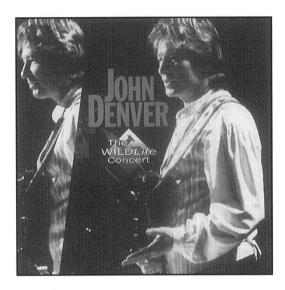